"This important book will inform, instruct, and inspire. Bob reminds us there's a reason behind our rejoicing, and there's substance beneath our singing. He patrols the theological borders of this book like a trusty Doberman who won't allow you to trespass into unhealthy attitudes and approaches in worship. But for all the *patrolling*, there's even more *pastoring*. As you read the pages of this book, be open to the whispers of the Holy Spirit. Be ready for him to guide you, remind you, realign you, or surprise you—for your greater good and his greater glory."

Matt Redman, recording artist; songwriter; Worship Leader,
Brighton, United Kingdom

"This book brings together years of experience, prayer, study, and discovery in a way that informs and inspires. For those passionate about growing deeper in their understanding of worship, this book is a fantastic and thought-provoking read!"

Tim Hughes, singer-songwriter; Director, Worship Central

"*True Worshipers* is an incredibly helpful book for understanding what it means to worship God. It goes beyond our sanctuaries and stages, but it always starts with God. And it always starts with our hearts. I am grateful for Bob Kauflin's refreshing honesty and humility as he shares from his experience. This book will be my first recommendation for those wanting to lead worship, as well as anyone seeking to deepen his or her relationship with God."

Lauren Chandler, author; songwriter; Worship Leader,
The Village Church, Flower Mound, Texas

"Bob Kauflin helps us prepare here and now for what we will spend an eternity doing in heaven—worshiping in spirit and in truth the One seated on the throne, singing the song of the Lamb. Nothing could be more important than this 'dress rehearsal' of worship."

Nancy Leigh DeMoss, author; radio host, *Revive Our Hearts*

"Bob Kauflin presents a balanced, mature, biblical understanding of worship. He is concerned above all for the heart—for the depth and authenticity of our relationship with God—which so often gets lost in the controversies over styles and traditions. I profited from this book, and in it Bob challenged the quality of my worship."

John M. Frame, J. D. Trimble Chair of Systematic Theology and Philosophy, Reformed Theological Seminary, Orlando, Florida

"With simplicity and clarity, Bob Kauflin tackles issues he has seen Christians struggle with in the years he has been a pastor, many of which relate to our gatherings. Bob confronts misconceptions about worship in an engaging way, relating everything to Scripture and incorporating helpful insights from other writers. Here is a book to put into the hands of any believer who is searching for answers about this vitally important topic."

David Peterson, former Principal, Oak Hill College; Senior Research Fellow and Lecturer in New Testament, Moore Theological College

"At a time when we so casually label all manner of products, conferences, and ministries with the modifier 'worship,' Bob's clear, practical, inspiring, and thoroughly biblical book brings us back to the heart of what is means to be a worshiper of God. Highly recommended."

Stuart Townend, Christian songwriter

"I am so thankful for the guidance Bob Kauflin gives us in *True Worshipers*. Bob writes as a pastor who understands what's at stake when we talk about worship, connecting our practices as the church gathered to the much bigger, all-of-life reality of worship. *True Worshipers* is a book for all Christians who want to deepen their practices as worshipers and deepen their intimacy with God."

Mike Cosper, Pastor of Worship and Arts, Sojourn Community Church, Louisville, Kentucky

"It's sad but true: while few things are more fundamental in our lives than worship, few things are more misunderstood. What *Worship Matters* did for worship leaders *True Worshipers* does for the rest of us—it draws our attention to what is most important when we think about worship. As a pastor, I'm grateful for the role this book will play in cultivating true worship in our church. As a Christian, I'm grateful this book challenges me to live my entire life delighting in, exalting, and serving the Savior. And as Bob's friend for the past four decades, I can tell you he is a compelling example of what is written on every page of this book."

C. J. Mahaney, Senior Pastor, Sovereign Grace Church of Louisville, Louisville, Kentucky

"Brilliant. Freeing. Needed. Worship is often limited to the walls of the church. In *True Worshipers*, Bob Kauflin reminds us that worship isn't a Sunday morning routine but rather an everyday lifestyle."

Louie Giglio, Pastor, Passion City Church, Atlanta, Georgia; Founder, the Passion Movement

"Bob Kauflin is a good friend who is always quick to encourage all that is good about writing, singing, and living the gospel. We encourage you to read anything he writes!"

Keith and Kristyn Getty, hymn writers; recording artists

TRUE WORSHIPERS

SEEKING
WHAT MATTERS
TO GOD

BOB KAUFLIN

FOREWORD BY MATT REDMAN

::: CROSSWAY

WHEATON, ILLINOIS

Trade paperback ISBN: 978-1-4335-4230-5
ePub ISBN: 978-1-4335-4233-6
PDF ISBN: 978-1-4335-4231-2
Mobipocket ISBN: 978-1-4335-4232-9

Library of Congress Cataloging-in-Publication Data
Kauflin, Bob.
True worshipers: seeking what matters to God / Bob Kauflin; foreword by Matt Redman.
    pages cm
  Includes bibliographical references and index.
  ISBN 978-1-4335-4230-5 (tp)
  ISBN 978-1-4335-4233-6 (ePub)
  ISBN 978-1-4335-4231-2 (PDF)
  ISBN 978-1-4335-4232-9 (Mobipocket)
  1. God—Worship and love—Biblical teaching. 2. God (Christianity)—Worship and love. 3. Christian life. I. Title.
BS680.W78K378   2015
264—dc23   2015003092

Crossway is a publishing ministry of Good News Publishers.

BP		25	24	23	22	21	20	19	18	17	16	15
15	14	13	12	11	10	9	8	7	6	5	4	3	2	1

To my children,

Megan, Jordan, Devon, Chelsea, Brittany, and McKenzie.

It has been one of the greatest joys of my life
to watch each of you become a true worshiper.

Proverbs 23:24

CONTENTS

FOREWORD

I first met Bob Kauflin at a UK seaside vacation resort, well over a decade ago. That might sound like a really nice setting to meet a new worship-leader friend, but believe me, it wasn't the place to be if you were looking for anything remotely resembling beach weather! The sea winds were howling, and I think the English rain was making fun of us. Fortunately, neither of us was there for a vacation. Instead, we were part of a gathering of several thousand worship leaders and their teams, and it was a powerful and profound conference.

I think what struck me most upon meeting Bob was his pursuit of *truth*. It comes as no surprise to me therefore that this new book has the title *True Worshipers*. On our first meeting, I remember Bob talking to me about the importance of biblical truth in our worship songs, and how essential it is for them to be full of God-honoring and Word-carrying lyrics. And Bob's passion for our worship to be biblically astute and our worship expressions to be theologically correct has shown up in so many different ways since.

I remember another conference we happened to be at together, and a question-and-answer session that followed the speaker's message. Bob's hand kept going up—and time after time he offered a passionate and purposeful comment or question around the theological theme we were discussing. As I look back on that day, it's almost like Bob was a crossbreed of theological Doberman and pastoral Labrador (which I mean as a huge compliment!). He went hard after biblical revelation and the defense of truth, but did so with much grace and love.

Bob does exactly the same in the pages of his excellent new book. He makes plain what worship is and what it isn't. He points us strongly in the right direction. But throughout every chapter, he does so with humility and care. If you're new to the topic of worship, you'll find some fantastic foundations to build your learning upon here. If you've been around this theme for a while, you'll find some timely reminders, and insights into age-old glorious truths. And all laid out in a helpful and well-thought-through way.

Worship is one of the ultimate themes of this life, but it is never a question of whether worship will or won't occur in the heart of a human being. It's more a case of whether that worship will travel in the proper direction and end up in the right place. It's guaranteed that everyone on this planet will be an extravagant worshiper of some kind, sacrificially spending themselves in a life of desire and devotion. But it's by no means guaranteed that their worship will travel along the right paths. People will find a way to worship anything and everything. But all the time, God is calling us back to himself, back to being the God reflectors and image bearers we were meant to be. He is the only One worthy of our worship. As C. S. Lewis reminded us, idols inevitably break the hearts of their worshipers. But not so when we worship

Jesus—of course the complete opposite occurs, and we find ourselves in a place of fulfillment and satisfaction.

One of the most reorienting passages in Scripture when it comes to the theme of worship is Revelation chapters 4 and 5. Here we see things set up as they were ever supposed to be. There in the center is the throne of God, and everything else (as Harold Best described it) arranges itself around that throne. We see a rainbow encircling that throne, and encounter a multitude of angels doing exactly the same thing—encircling the throne of Jesus. That is a picture of how our lives should look here on earth, just as is in heaven. We are meant to gather ourselves around the throne of God and make sure Jesus is absolutely central to the way we arrange our lives.

Some will read this book and realize that Christ has recently been placed a little off-center in their lives. They'll see how, perhaps in subtle ways, some other person or factor has started to take too central a place. There'll be some rearranging of the furniture to do, with Jesus and his throne being moved back to the very heart of who we are. Others will have a similar epiphany in terms of how they see the worship-music ministry God has entrusted to them. Perhaps outward things have become too dominant and there's a call to readjust and find a renewed heart of worship. As you read the pages of this book, be open to the whispers of the Holy Spirit. Be ready for him to guide you, remind you, realign you, or surprise you—for your greater good and his greater glory.

This important book will inform, instruct, and inspire. Bob reminds us there's a reason behind our rejoicing, and there's substance beneath our singing. And ultimately he encourages us to back up anything we sing or say with a life of exuberant and God-focused worship. Back to my (hopefully not offensive!) dog analogy—Bob patrols the theological borders of this book like that trusty Doberman who won't allow you to trespass into unhealthy attitudes and approaches in worship. But for all the *patrolling*, there's even more *pastoring*—Bob's Labrador side accompanying all this teaching with gentleness, humility, patience, and much care.

I'm glad to have met Bob all those years ago and to have benefited from his wisdom, experience, and passion for exalting Christ. I know by the end of this book you will feel exactly the same way.

Matt Redman

ACKNOWLEDGMENTS

I owe a significant debt of gratitude to many people whose lives, directly or indirectly, influenced and shaped what I wrote in this work.

To Lane Dennis, for the privilege of writing another book for Crossway, still one of my favorite publishers. The books you've produced have been a huge means of grace to my life.

To Justin Taylor, for supporting, encouraging, and prodding me during the six years it took me to write this book. You are kind, generous, thoughtful, and superhumanly patient.

To Thomas Womack and Thom Notaro, for lending your excellent editing capabilities to this book. Thomas, it was a joy to benefit from your wise and insightful gifts again, and Thom, it was a pleasure to work with you for the first time.

To Amy Kruis, Angie Cheatham, Dan Bush, Danny Lee, Matt Tully, and all the other folks at Crossway who helped produce *True Worshipers*, and more importantly, who provide the church with gospel-centered, theologically rich, Christ-exalting books.

To D. A. Carson, David Peterson, John Piper, and Harold Best, for writing books that helped me appreciate the importance of understanding God, engaging with God, desiring God, and knowing how to use music to glorify God.

To the staff of Sovereign Grace Churches, whose unseen, faithful labors are being used by God to advance the gospel, build churches, and encourage true worshipers throughout the world.

To Joseph Stigora, Matthew Williams, Walt Alexander, Erik Schmaltz, Jason Hansen, Tim Payne, Jon Bloom, and Doug Plank, for helping me equip Sovereign Grace Churches in knowing how to use music in the church to exalt Christ.

To my fellow pastors in Sovereign Grace Churches, who every week seek to teach, equip, and deploy the true worshipers under your care to make a difference for the gospel in your community and beyond.

To the Boyce College and the Southern Baptist Theological Seminary interns I have the privilege of hanging with. You've helped me work through many of the thoughts in this book. Thanks for your engaging conversations, insightful comments, and enthusiastic support.

To Jon Payne, Matt Mason, Jordan and Devon (my sons), and anyone else who gave me feedback on this book as it was in process. Your thoughts were invaluable and made this a better book than it would have been otherwise.

To the pastors and members of Sovereign Grace Church of Louisville. It is a gift from God to be able to labor beside you for the glory of the Savior. Your humble and consistent example of being true worshipers inspires and gladdens my soul.

To Brittany, my daughter/assistant, who keeps me on schedule, tries to keep me from over-scheduling, and has been gifted with seemingly endless creativity. Because your life sings with the joy of the gospel, you make me one of the happiest bosses and dads I know.

To Jeff Purswell. I could never have imagined the impact you would have on my life when we first started serving together back in 1997. Thank you for the theological precision, literary clarity, and stylistic improvements you brought to this book. You made me ask hard questions, and I'm grateful for it. More importantly, thank you for helping me, through your teaching and friendship, to treasure, submit to, and apply the Word of God.

To C. J. Mahaney. This book (and my first one) wouldn't exist apart from your example, teaching, and friendship. You are one of the finest examples of a true worshiper I know. You walk humbly with your God, exult in grace, are continually in awe that Jesus died in your place, and live in the power of the Spirit. Thank you for poring through the pages of this book with me and suggesting so many ways it could be better. It's eternally significant that you're a true worshiper, but I thank God that you're also a true pastor and a true friend.

To my children and their spouses—Megan and James, Jordan and Tali, Devon and Kristine, Chelsea and Jacob, Brittany, and McKenzie. Thank you for your desire to bring glory to Jesus Christ not only through your songs but through your lives. May you experience the unspeakable blessing of having your children, too, grow up to be true worshipers.

To my dearest Julie, the most amazing human being I know. Thank you for being so supportive and encouraging as I wrote, rewrote, and wrote again this book. Thanks for telling me to stay late and work when I knew we'd both rather be together. Thank you for always pointing my eyes and heart to our faithful Father, our merciful Savior, and the ever-present Holy Spirit. Thank you for saying yes back in 1976. It just keeps getting better.

Finally, to the God and Savior whom I grew to know and love more deeply while writing this book. Any words I write are inevitably inadequate to express the praise you're due. Your majesty is unparalleled, your beauty unsurpassed, your wisdom unmeasured, your goodness unimaginable, your steadfast love unchanging, and your greatness unsearchable. I consider it the greatest end of my existence to find myself numbered among those worshiping the One on the throne and the Lamb. I pray that as a result of reading this book, many more will say the same.

1

TRUE WORSHIPERS *MATTER*

WORSHIP AND REALITY

> But the hour is coming, and is now here, when the true worshipers will worship the Father in spirit and truth, for the Father is seeking such people to worship him.
>
> JOHN 4:23

The year was 1975. I was standing in an open field next to my future wife, Julie, in Front Royal, Virginia. Along with a few thousand other people, we had come to experience Fishnet, one of the first outdoor "Jesus festivals." More specifically, we had come to experience the music.

Converted rock bands, singer-songwriters, and folk musicians had started singing about Jesus without missing a beat. And their songs were making their way into the church. "Worship," as we started calling it, became almost indistinguishable from what was being played on the radio. Traditionalists questioned and feared it. Young people devoured it.

Fishnet and festivals like it were the first signs that a worship tidal wave was about to crash upon the shores of the church. Conversations about worship then were relatively few. In just a few years, "worship" would hit the big time.

IT'S A WORSHIP WORLD

Decades later, an ever-increasing number of books, magazines, websites, and blogs are devoted exclusively to the topic of worship, or at least worship music. Worship has become a *thing*, if not *the* thing. It's a movement, a phenomenon, and in many places, an industry.

There have been undeniable benefits. This heightened focus on worship has produced resources that help us think about it in a more biblical and comprehensive way.[1] The outpouring of new worship songs has been astounding. Although most will be forgotten, some modern hymns show signs of being around for decades, if not centuries. Congregational singing has been revitalized, and a new generation of musicians are being raised up to use their gifts for the church. Young people now fill large arenas to worship God with songs that unabashedly proclaim a passion for Jesus Christ.

But it hasn't all been good. Heated arguments about worship-music styles have divided or destroyed congregations. Performance is often valued over participation, and technology over truth. Many songs have been written by musicians who don't know their Bibles very well, resulting in songs that lack gospel and theological clarity. Worst of all, worship has been reduced almost universally to what happens when we sing.

Whether you see the "worship phenomenon" as a good thing, a bad thing, or somewhere in between, this much is certain: the worship of God matters. It's never irrelevant. It's never unimportant. The worship of God should *always be* a hot topic. And from God's perspective, it is. There is nothing more foundational to our relationship with God and to our lives as Christians.

And not surprisingly, we're not the first generation of Christians to think about it.

THE END OF OUR EXISTENCE

"We should consider it the great end of our existence to be found numbered among the worshipers of God."[2] These words first appeared over 450 years ago, penned by the French theologian and pastor John Calvin. He wasn't imagining a guitar-driven band playing the latest worship hits, or a pipe organ accompanying a choir. I don't think music was even on his mind. But his words are as relevant to us today as they were to his original audience. And they sum up why I wrote this book.

Most of us don't give "the great end of our existence" much thought. The duties, distractions, joys, trials, and temptations of this life are more than sufficient to keep our minds occupied every waking moment. Consider eternity? We don't have the time.

When we do think about the afterlife, we often look forward to things like being reunited with loved ones, singing our favorite worship songs endlessly, devouring all the chocolate we want without gaining weight, or playing unlimited rounds of golf on the perfect course. Atheists say we're simply going to cease to exist, so there's nothing "great" about it. We just die.

As a Christian, I believe Calvin's words are true for all of us, religious or not. He isn't saying that everyone *will* be found numbered among the worshipers of God. Rather, he's encouraging us to see this as our highest goal, our loftiest aim—the great purpose of our existence. Better than having all the power, wealth, talent, intelligence, or pleasure you could ever imagine is being a worshiper of God forever.

I suspect worshiping God is at least on your radar, given that you're reading this. More likely, your relationship with God has only stirred your desire to know him in deeper ways. Your love for God has only made you want to love him more.

Maybe you've been unexpectedly overcome with gratefulness while singing with your church. Perhaps you've sensed God's presence so strongly at times that you wanted to kneel down in silent awe. Or in the middle of reading your Bible one morning it struck you how amazing Jesus is, and you were undone. Maybe while you were studying, working hard, or caring for a friend, you realized you were doing it for God's glory, not your own, and it felt oh so good.

I've experienced all these things and more. When I do experience them, I'm grateful that at least for the moment, I'm wholly focused on the God who redeemed me. And at those times, I think, yes, it *is* the great end of our existence to be numbered among the worshipers of God. For all eternity.

WORSHIP THEN . . . AND NOW

But being numbered among the worshipers of God *then* and being numbered among them *now* are two very different things. In this life, worship isn't always what it could be. And you might be thinking, *In my experience, it's never what it could be!*

I get it. I've been a Christian for more than forty years and have known the highs and lows of what it means to be a worshiper of God. I'm also aware that the idea of worship, depending on who you ask, can sound incredibly exciting, unspeakably boring, mildly confusing, or at best, irrelevant. For some, the word *worship* is pregnant with eager expectation; others have to stifle a yawn.

However you define it, we can all struggle with worshiping God this side of heaven. Maybe you can identify with some of these perspectives:

- Worshiping God is difficult, if not impossible, due to your challenging circumstances, unfulfilled hopes, or ongoing suffering. Your experience seems to contradict God's goodness.
- You're not totally clear on how Sunday morning worship relates to worship in everyday life.
- You've seen tensions rise because of the music we connect with worship. Conflicts erupt, musicians seek the spotlight, churches split. You wonder if music is overblown.
- You've seen the music we connect with worship affect unbelievers, strengthen the impact of biblical truth, and deepen people's responses to God. You wonder if music is undervalued.
- The "great end of our existence" seems insignificant when it comes to the pressures, demands, and responsibilities you face every day.

I'm sure you can add to this list. But even with all these challenges and questions, John Calvin was right. We can have no higher goal than to take our place among those who revel—unceasingly, joyfully, wholeheartedly, and eternally—in our great and awesome God. That's where every Christian is headed, according to the Bible's last chapter: "No longer will there be anything accursed, but the throne of God and of the Lamb will be in it, and his servants will worship him" (Rev. 22:3).

So if eternal worship is where we're headed, what does it mean for us now? Does it make any difference? What does it even mean to be a worshiper of God? I hope to answer these questions and more in this book. And to start, I want to drop in on a familiar conversation that took place two thousand years ago.

A WOMAN AND A WELL

It's a sweltering, dusty day somewhere in the Middle East, and Jesus is thirsty. He sits down at a well to wait for a woman from Samaria he's never met.[3]

Give me a drink.

It's a simple request. But those four words cross religious, ethnic, and moral lines that have been in place for generations. The woman is dumbfounded.

How is it that you, a Jew, ask for a drink from me, a woman of Samaria?

She has good reason to wonder. In the eighth century BC, Assyria conquered the Samaritans and brought in idolaters from other nations to intermarry with them. Since that time, the rest of the Jews have viewed Samaritans as half-breeds, religious mutts. They are people you avoid, not pursue. They use an edited Bible and worship God at a different temple.

On top of that, Jesus is a man. Jewish men are never to be overly familiar with women, and speaking to a woman alone would look very suspicious. Jesus is undeterred.

If you knew the gift of God, and who it is that is saying to you, "Give me a drink," you would have asked him, and he would have given you living water.

Jesus doesn't answer the woman's question. He's not even asking her for a drink anymore. He's offering her one. He wants her to see that she's the one who needs water. Living water. Jesus goes on to make an uncomfortably perceptive comment about the woman's home life.

You have had five husbands, and the one you now have is not your husband.

It's not often a man you just met unveils the scandalous details of your life. She discerns that Jesus must be a prophet. Maybe he even knows the answer to a question that has divided Jews and Samaritans for centuries. A question about worship.

Our fathers worshiped on this mountain, but you say that in Jerusalem is the place where people ought to worship.

At this point the woman may be trying to turn the spotlight away from her personal affairs. Maybe she genuinely wants to resolve the ongoing debate. It's even possible she holds out hope she can somehow deal with her sin. But it doesn't matter. This time, Jesus answers her question.

Woman, believe me, the hour is coming when neither on this mountain nor in Jerusalem will you worship the Father. You worship what you do not know; we worship what we know, for salvation is from the Jews.

Jesus tells the woman her knowledge of worship is woefully deficient. Earthly geography is a fading category. She doesn't even know the one she claims to worship. And that's after he's already introduced the disconnect between her life and her professed religion. He goes on.

The hour is coming, and is now here, when the true worshipers will worship the Father in spirit and truth, for the Father is seeking such people to worship him.

Spirit and truth? The Father seeking? It's a typical Jesus response—unexpected, enigmatic, and containing implications far beyond what the woman could have dreamed. Implications that reach to you and me.

● ● ●

The fact that Jesus had this conversation with an immoral woman in an obscure village should tell us something. God isn't seeking worshipers only among the significant and popular people, the successful and powerful ones. The Maker of the universe is seeking true worshipers among us all.

But why is God *seeking* something? Surely the all-knowing, all-seeing One doesn't lose things. And it's not as though a self-sufficient God has any needs. Why would God seek anything?

We seek what's important to us. We seek what has value. And God is seeking true worshipers—because true worshipers matter to God.

WHAT'S AHEAD

For those of us who think of worship primarily in terms of musically driven emotional experiences, Jesus's conversation with the Samaritan woman should be eye-opening. Jesus is talking about "true worshipers" and he doesn't reference music once. Not a whisper of bands, organs, keyboards, choirs, drum sets, guitars, or even lutes, lyres, and timbrels.

Can we find out what it means to be a true worshiper and not talk about music? Apparently. We'll get to music, but we don't start with it. Music is a part of worshiping God, but it was never meant to be the heart of it.

"True worshipers," Jesus told the woman, are those who "worship the Father in spirit and truth." He went on to say more emphatically that "God is spirit, and those who worship him *must* worship in spirit and truth" (John 4:24). Broadly speaking, worship in spirit and truth is worship that springs from a sincere heart and lines up with the truth of God's Word. But there's more to what Jesus was saying.

To worship God *in truth*, says New Testament scholar D. A. Carson, "is first and foremost a way of saying that we must worship God *by means of Christ*. In him the reality has dawned and the shadows are being swept away."[4] And Jesus is the one who gives the life-giving Spirit, who produces rivers of living water in a believer's soul (John 7:38–39). It's the Spirit who brings life to our spirits and enables us to know, love, and worship God the Father through Jesus Christ.

In other words, it takes God to worship God.

So that's where we'll start. Jesus told the Samaritan woman not only that the Father was *seeking* true worshipers, but that he came to *make* her one. Her story is the story of every true worshiper. We begin by acknowledging our inability to worship God unless he draws us by his grace and reveals himself to us through his Word.

From that vantage point, we'll talk about the essence of worshiping God, which is exalting him in our hearts and actions. Any definition of true worship that denies or minimizes God's supremacy, authority, and uniqueness is unbiblical and will lead to idolatry.

While God calls us individually to be true worshipers, he has always planned to have a *people* who would bring him glory in this life and the next (Ex. 19:5–6; 1 Pet. 2:9–10). So we'll take time to talk about the history and benefits of gathering with those God has redeemed, the community of worship.

Worship is *ultimately* about God, but it's not *solely* about God. God wants to receive glory as we serve others with our gifts. In fact, that's one of the primary reasons we gather. As we exercise our gifts, God is in our midst building us up both as individuals and as a local church. So we'll spend time talking about the horizontal aspects of worshiping God.

One of those horizontal aspects is the sometimes troubling, often tempting, ever-timeless area of music, especially singing. Probably because I've been leading congregational song for thirty-five years, I'll spend two chapters on music. The first focuses on why God wants us to sing together, and the second addresses challenges that often arise.

Worshiping God is often associated with his presence. But what does it look like for God's Spirit to dwell among us? Should we expect in some way to be aware of what he's doing? How can we "seek his presence continually," as we're instructed to do in Psalm 105:4, without losing our biblical moorings and becoming driven by emotion? We'll look at those questions and more as we consider God's activity among us and what it means to encounter him.

Finally, we'll reflect on what Calvin encourages us to consider as the great end of our existence: to be found numbered among the worshipers of God in eternity. In his first letter, Peter tells his readers, "Set your hope fully on the grace that will be brought to you at the revelation of Jesus Christ" (1 Pet. 1:13). That's what we'll begin to do in the final chapter as we reflect on worship in the new age, both what we can see now and the unimaginable joys that await us.

WORSHIP RIGHT SIDE UP

I have to confess I wanted to write a longer book. I wanted to explore how being a true worshiper relates to topics like prayer, evangelism, the sacraments, ministry to the poor, Bible study, spiritual disciplines, and more. But a longer book would probably mean fewer people would read it. So I resisted.

What I've tried to do is focus on areas I've seen Christians struggle with in the thirty years I've been a pastor, many of which relate to our gatherings. They happen to be areas I've struggled with as well.

In many ways we're a lot like the Samaritan woman Jesus encountered. She didn't know God as well as she thought. She had a hard time connecting gathered worship and her daily life. She struggled with where and how God could be worshiped. And she questioned who she was supposed to worship with.

The words Jesus spoke to her speak to us as well. He helps us see that worship begins with God's extravagant grace, not our earnest efforts. He shows us that he is the center of true worship, however much our thinking might be sidetracked by personal preferences, emotional experiences, and religious traditions. He introduces us to unseen realities that fulfill us deeply and eternally, freeing us from bondage to things we can see that satisfy only temporarily.

The Samaritan woman thought she understood worship. But her understanding was radically altered by her encounter with Jesus at a well. How would we respond if Jesus wanted to alter *our* understanding of worship? To turn it upside down—or better, right side up? Is it possible that rather than looking for something *from* us, God first has something to *give* us?

Could it be that worship doesn't even begin with us?

TRUE WORSHIPERS *RECEIVE*

WORSHIP AND OUR INABILITY

What do you have that you did not receive? If then you
received it, why do you boast as if you did not receive it?

1 CORINTHIANS 4:7

I have a good friend named Craig who years ago attended
seminary, carrying a heavy class load and serving in an unpaid
internship. Being a typical seminary student, he was dirt poor.

Craig kept in touch with a college buddy who'd landed a
job that actually paid good money. Every so often, the two
of them enjoyed a meal at a local restaurant. Despite Craig's
genuine protests, the friend would always foot the bill. Finally, Craig took a stand. "Please let me pay!" he insisted.

His friend was unmoved. "Craig, why is it so hard for you
to receive? You can't even be a *Christian* if you can't receive!"

Craig's friend was right. Our first responsibility as Christians is not to give to God but to receive from him. More

emphatically, we can say that when it comes to being a true worshiper, receiving from God is our calling from first to last.

There are two aspects to our receiving. First, we need to be invited and enabled. We're powerless to come to God in our own strength. Second, God must show us what he's really like. Jesus said, "No one knows the Father except the Son and anyone to whom the Son chooses to reveal him" (Matt. 11:27). We can't figure God out on our own. As with the Samaritan woman, God must reveal himself to us before we can respond to him rightly.

Receiving the gift of a meal is a choice between being polite or rude. But receiving the gift of worship is a matter of life or death. God makes that clear throughout Scripture, from the very beginning.

THE FIRST WORSHIPERS

The Bible opens with the words "In the beginning, *God*." Not "In the beginning, *Adam*" or "In the beginning, *animals*" or "In the beginning, *a gaseous cloud*."

In the beginning, *God* . . .

Before anything came to be, God was. Exuberantly happy, completely content, incomprehensibly radiant, and dwelling "in unapproachable light" (1 Tim. 6:16). The Father, Son, and Holy Spirit unceasingly delighting in each other's perfections from eternity past (John 17:5, 24).[1] Out of his desire to display his glory and have us share in his joy, God acted. He created a universe, a galaxy called the Milky Way, our solar system, a planet called Earth, and a place called Eden.

Eden was an idyllic environment. No sin. No imperfection. No decay or defilement. Paradise. But it wasn't the environment that made Eden so special. It was the Presence. The first couple lived in a world ablaze with God's presence and glory. Adam and Eve instinctively knew why they had been made. They breathed, ate, slept, played, and labored to exalt the goodness and greatness of God.

D. A. Carson explains that in this time before the fall,

> God's image-bearers delighted in the perfection of his creation and the pleasure of his presence precisely because they were perfectly oriented toward him. No redemptive provisions had yet been disclosed, for none were needed. There was no need to exhort human beings to worship; their entire existence revolved around the God who had made them.[2]

Our first parents were born worshiping. But when they ate the forbidden fruit, their worship was redirected. Duped by a serpent, they rejected the gift of worshiping God and chose to worship themselves. They thought God could be improved upon. They were wrong. And as a result of their decision, all creation plunged into futility and despair.

Ashamed, confused, and afraid, Adam and Eve tried to hide their nakedness and rebellion from God. But God came seeking. Rather than put them to death, which he had every right to do, God covered Adam and Eve with animal skins. God drew the first drop of blood in his creation. For us. He sought us out and provided for us when all we wanted to do was run from him.

UNABLE ON OUR OWN

Throughout Scripture, our need for God to enable our worship is evident at every step. Cain and Abel both bring an offering to the Lord, but only Abel's is accepted. As we learn later, it's because Abel comes in faith, trusting not in his own efforts but in God (Heb. 11:4). Cain is inconsolable, and the first recorded worship service results in one worshiper killing the other.

God continues to invite and pursue. He rescues Noah and his family through the flood, and hope is momentarily restored. But before long the Tower of Babel proves again that our worship compass has gone awry.

Years later, God calls Abraham out of pagan Ur and promises that his descendants will outnumber the stars (Gen. 12:2; 15:5). Abraham is stunned. And as God enables barren Sarah to conceive a son, our inability and God's grace are on full display.

After Israel spends four hundred years in Egypt, much of it as slaves, Moses attempts to deliver them, fails, and then escapes to the desert to tend sheep for forty years. There in a burning bush, God reveals himself to Moses as the self-sufficient "I AM" (Ex. 3:14). "I will take you to be my people, and I will be your God, and you shall know that I am the LORD your God, who has brought you out from under the burdens of the Egyptians" (Ex. 6:7). God's initiative is pervasive: "I will take you . . . I will be . . . I am the LORD . . . who has brought you out."

Once he's delivered them, God meets with his people at Mount Sinai. He provides laws to obey and sacrifices to offer when they disobey. Both are gracious gifts, enabling them to draw near a holy God without being consumed.

In the centuries to follow, God sends prophet after prophet to reveal his character and commands to the Israelites. Despite countless initiatives, Israel continues to lust after idols rather than find refuge in their husband and Maker (Isa. 54:5).

The Old Testament ends not with jubilant celebration but with the painful realization that all our efforts to bring glory to God result in failure and condemnation. If God is to have a people who will worship him with all their heart, soul, mind, and strength, he will have to bring it about himself.

After four hundred years, he does. Jesus is born. In an act of unfathomable love, Deity becomes dust, the Maker becomes the maligned, the Creator becomes the cursed. God comes in Christ to restore the relationship we rejected in the garden. We learn that the greatest gift God gives us is himself.

Jesus is God's ultimate statement that he will provide a way for us to worship him—not only in this life but for all eternity. Where our offerings are tainted with self-reliance and self-exaltation, Jesus empties himself to bring glory to his Father on our behalf. Jesus's perfect life, substitutionary death on the cross, physical resurrection, and glorious ascension assure once and for all that those who trust in him can be numbered among the worshipers of God.

For thousands of years since then, God has been seeking all those willing to receive the gift of worshiping him. In his sovereign mercy, I turned out to be one of them.

AN UNWELCOME GUEST

Unlike his appearing to Moses, God didn't speak to me in the desert through a burning bush. It was far more mundane. God met me in a college student union building through a faithful Christian I wanted to avoid.

Every so often, this guy—I don't remember his name, so I'll call him Jim—would stop by my dorm room to engage in small talk. Somehow, the conversation always led to spiritual topics. Jim was from Campus Crusade for Christ, now known as Cru. I could tell he was unimpressed with my spirituality and wanted to talk about it.

In my eyes, I was already spiritual. I read the New Testament almost every night and prayed before meals. As a high school freshman I attended a junior seminary meant to prepare me for the Catholic priesthood. It closed down due to declining enrollment, but I maintained a spiritual mind-set for the rest of high school. I didn't drink, curse, do drugs, or sleep with girls. I went to church every Sunday.

I was so spiritual that in eighth grade I had started writing a book I humbly called *Six Easy Steps to Being Perfect*. Really.

In any case, I was definitely spiritual. But apparently not spiritual enough for Jim. So I finally agreed to meet with him one night in the fall of my freshman year, figuring I'd politely listen and maybe even set him straight on a few things.

AN UNEXPECTED GIFT

My recollections of the conversation that night are hazy. But there's one part I'll never forget. After a few minutes, Jim pulled out a Bible.

"Have you ever read this verse?" he asked.

For all have sinned and fall short of the glory of God (Rom. 3:23).

Yes, I'd read it. And I thought the meaning was obvious. Of course I'd sinned. I knew I wasn't perfect, and I didn't claim to be, my book-writing project notwithstanding. As our conversation continued, I got the distinct sense that falling short of the glory of God was worse than I'd thought.

Jim took me to another verse.

For the wages of sin is death . . . (Rom. 6:23).

Throughout my life I reasoned that as long as I did my best and got to confession when I didn't, God would show me mercy. He'd have to let me into heaven when I died. But the truth was, I never did my best. Ever. I was not only relying on my own "goodness," but constantly falling short even of my *own* standards.

It wasn't that I didn't know what God wanted. I knew exactly what he wanted and prided myself on keeping a few rules while ignoring or failing to obey countless others. I should have been dead. But I wasn't.

For the first time in my life, I began to see how radically different God's perspective was from mine. I thought of myself as a sincere guy with a few issues. God saw me as a rebel, openly defying his good and just laws. Nothing I'd done or could do would ever change my status before him. He was holy, I was unholy. He was pure, I was defiled. He was the righteous Judge, I was the condemned sinner.

We looked at the rest of that verse.

. . . but the free gift of God is eternal life in Jesus Christ our Lord.

Up until that night I thought favor with God was ultimately something I had to earn through doing good deeds and avoiding bad ones. But here God was saying eternal life is a gift.

To press the point home, Jim handed me a pencil. "This is my gift to you. It's yours." I had no idea where he was going with this. Then he asked, "Did you do anything to earn that gift?"

No.

"Did you pay for that gift?"

No.

"Am I going to take that gift away from you?"

No.

A light began to dawn. The meaning of the cross was becoming clearer. Jesus came to die in my place to give me a *gift*. Not something I had to earn, prove myself worthy of, or labor to keep. A gift.

Jesus actually did the best he could. And it was perfect. No flaws, no failures, no sins—secret or open. Then he took upon himself the punishment I deserved for all *my* sins, past, present, and future. The wrath of God fell upon him instead of me. He cried out, "My God, my God, why have you forsaken me?" so I would never have to.

It's what the hymn writer expressed when he wrote,

My sin—oh, the bliss of this glorious thought—
my sin, not in part but the whole,
is nailed to the cross and I bear it no more;
praise the Lord, praise the Lord, O my soul![3]

It's what God himself tells us in his Word: "He himself bore our sins in his body on the tree, that we might die to sin and live to righteousness. By his wounds you have been healed" (1 Pet. 2:24).

Through his death in my place Jesus overcame everything that would keep me from heaven—sin, death, demons, and hell. If I turned from my self-exalting, self-consumed way of life and believed Christ's death completely paid the debt I owed to God, I would be forgiven. Reconciled to God. Adopted into his family. Forever.

It sounded too good to be true. But grace always does. We come to God by grace or we don't come at all. We come by receiving a gift, not by doing a deed. We don't create worship; we respond to what we've received in Jesus Christ—eternal life. And that gift continues to be the basis upon which we come to worship God.

That's why Paul reminds Titus, "When the goodness and loving kindness of God our Savior appeared, he saved us, not because of works done by us in righteousness, but according to his own mercy" (Titus 3:4–5). Mercy that's deserved is no longer mercy.

And worship that doesn't begin with mercy is no longer worship.

REVELATION AND RESPONSE

The ability and desire to worship God is something that God himself gives us. But there's another aspect to that gift. In the process of drawing and enabling us, God reveals himself to us. He tells us who he is. Not only are we unable to worship God apart from his grace; we don't even know who it is we're worshiping. God has to tell us. And he's done that in the Bible.

That night when I met with Jim, it wasn't his persuasive powers or his excellent communication skills that changed me. God used Jim, but it was the Spirit of God speaking through the Word of God that opened my eyes to see. God's Word revealed what his holiness required of me, how far I fell short, and how God himself came in Jesus Christ to fulfill what he required.

Worship that's acceptable to God, writes theologian Derek Kidner, "must be more than flattery and more than guess-work. It is the loving homage of the committed to the Revealed."[4] Our worship of God begins with God revealing himself to us and is sustained by that revelation. British pastor Vaughan Roberts fills out that thought:

> Worship never begins with us; it is always a response to the truth. It flows out of an understanding of who God is and what he has done for us in Christ. It begins with his revelation and redemption. So we must ensure that the Bible, which contains that revelation and points us to God's work of redemption, stays right at the heart of our meetings and our own spiritual lives.[5]

If God didn't reveal himself to us, we wouldn't know who to trust, who to obey, who to thank, or who to serve. We wouldn't know what God is like, what he has commanded, or what he has promised. Most importantly, we wouldn't know how he brought us near to himself and into his family through the substitutionary sacrifice of his Son on the cross. And all those truths are necessary to know if we want to worship God for who he is.

True worship is *always* a response to God's Word. John Stott has wisely said: "God must speak to us before we have any liberty to speak to him. He must disclose to us who he is before we can offer him what we are in acceptable worship. The worship of God is always a response to the Word of God. Scripture wonderfully directs and enriches our worship."[6] God's Word always directs and enriches our worship of God. But more than that, it's foundational. We can't worship God apart from his Word. It defines, directs, and inspires our worship. Scripture provides doctrinal fuel for our emotional fire.

Knowing God through his Word enables us to receive what we need to worship him.

CLEARING UP SOME COMMON MISCONCEPTIONS

But some Christians have difficulty connecting the worship of God with the Word of God. They wonder, *Isn't worship more about emotions than about words? Don't people just argue about the Bible? Isn't worship more about the Spirit? Why is the Bible so hard to understand?*

Each of these questions reveals a misconception about how God's Word is a gift from God that enables us to worship him. Left unanswered, they'll keep us from receiving the riches of grace God invites us to enjoy through his Word. Let's consider them one at a time.

Misconception 1: Worship is more about emotions than about words. I once met a husband and wife whose relationship had a unique start. He spoke English; she spoke Russian. Once they realized they were attracted to one another, they knew that looks, emotions, and gestures were an inadequate foundation for a potential marriage partner. So one of them learned to speak the other's language. Meaningful relationships require words.

So it is that when God invites us into a relationship with himself, he uses words. They're found in the Bible.

Scripture isn't made up of isolated verses that have some magical quality in and of themselves. Taken together and empowered by God's Spirit, they are his communicating with us, telling us what he's like. But the Bible doesn't just tell us *about* God; God is actually speaking to us (Heb. 4:12). The Word of God is the primary way God begins and deepens our relationship with him, and is essential for true worship.

Worship certainly involves more than words, and there will be times we worship God without words. But even then, "our only access to a real relationship with the living God in which words sometimes fall away is precisely in and through words which God speaks to us."[7]

Many Christians think of preaching as a "mind thing" and worship as a "heart thing." They'd be happy if the sermon was cut back so more time could be given to "worship," meaning the singing. The same attitude can be reflected in a dislike for songs that are "wordy," or a mind-set that says reading Scripture "interrupts" worship.

Now it might be that the preaching in your church is subpar while the music is outstanding. But God's Word— reading it, studying it, preaching it, hearing it, praying it, and singing it—is indispensable to the true worshipers God seeks. Knowing our Bibles well doesn't deaden our worship of God but rather informs and enflames it. God will always be much better than anything we could imagine him to be on our own.

If we want to grow as true worshipers of God, we won't simply listen to more music—we'll seek to encounter him in our Bibles.

Misconception 2: People just argue about the Bible. Years ago a leader at a conference asked us to shout out the names of our denominations. An indistinguishable roar erupted. Then he had us shout out the name of the head of the church. "Jesus!" we all proclaimed in unison. "See?" he said. "Doctrine divides us. Jesus unites us."

While I appreciated the leader's intent to honor Jesus, his conclusion actually dishonored him and was seriously misguided. *Doctrine* is a word meaning "something that is taught." It refers to everything the Bible teaches on a particular topic, such as worship, holiness, or the end times. Everyone has doctrine. Your doctrine is good if it affirms and lines up with what the Bible actually teaches. Your doctrine is bad if it doesn't.

Christians have disagreed over doctrinal issues of secondary importance for centuries. That's no surprise, given our sinful hearts and Satan's desire to separate us. But the New Testament warned that false teachers would infiltrate the church's ranks (Acts 20:29–30; 2 Cor. 11:13). Many of the most precious truths we live by today were more clearly defined as a response to heresy. The truths of the Christian faith have often been tested and confirmed in the fires of controversy and conflict.

People argue about the Bible because what's in it is a matter of life and death. To begin with, God has revealed himself to us as Father, Son, and Spirit, three persons existing in one God. He has revealed himself most fully to us in Jesus, the second person of the Trinity, who existed before time with the Father and Holy Spirit. Everything was created through him. He was born of a virgin, lived a perfect life of obedience to God, and endured God's wrath against the sins of all those who would trust in him. He was raised physically from the dead and ascended to his Father's right hand. He has poured out the Holy Spirit on those who trust in him, and he will one day return triumphantly to live with his bride, the church, forever.

In other words, it's misinformed to think that if we just worship God, everything else is unimportant or will work itself out. Unless we read our Bibles well, we won't know the God we're worshiping. When we fail to be specific about who God is and what he's done, we're really saying we want our own God. But true worship isn't based on our personal opinions, ideas, experiences, best guesses, or some lowest common denominator.

As author Michael Horton reminds us, "Vagueness about the object of our praise inevitably leads to making our own praise the object. Praise therefore becomes an end in itself, and we are caught up in our own 'worship experience' rather than in the God whose character and acts are the only proper focus."[8]

Worship given to a God we aren't willing to define ends up being a product of our own imagination, not a gift from God.

Misconception 3: Worship is more about the Spirit than about the Word. In his letter to the Philippians, Paul writes that Christians are those who "worship by the Spirit of God" (Phil. 3:3). He's affirming what we've been discussing in this chapter—that we've been brought into God's family through the working of God's Spirit, not through our own efforts or merit.

But for years I thought Paul was saying (and I'm not alone on this) that worship "in the Spirit" meant spontaneous singing, heightened emotions, and the pursuit of experiences. Perhaps you've thought something similar. I've been to meetings, and even led them, where the goal of the evening was to sing songs and allow the Holy Spirit to move among his people and do whatever he wanted. Sometimes they're referred to as "Holy Spirit nights." During such times we tend to minimize or mistrust Scripture, planning, and order.

There's no dichotomy between God's Spirit and God's Word. The Spirit is the one who gave us the Scripture in the first place: "All Scripture is *breathed out* by God and profitable for teaching, for reproof, for correction, and for training in righteousness" (2 Tim. 3:16). The phrase "breathed out" is a clear reference to the Spirit's work in authoring the words of the Bible through human instruments.

That means our "Spirit-filled worship" is to be evaluated by and submitted to what God has revealed in the Bible. The Spirit is integrally and inseparably connected to his Word.

Every church or individual Christian who claims to be Spirit-led must be Word-fed. If we want to know more of the Spirit's power in our lives, we would be wise to fill ourselves with the riches of his Word.

Misconception 4: The Bible is too hard to understand. Sometimes we think we should be able to understand God like a cake recipe or a sixth-grade textbook. But if we could grasp God easily or completely, he would no longer be worthy of our worship. He would no longer be God. When Scripture uses words like *unsearchable*, *inscrutable*, and *immeasurable* to describe God (as in Ps. 145:3; Rom. 11:33; Eph. 1:19), we should anticipate that our minds will be stretched to their limits as we seek to know him.

Studying God in his Word can seem laborious, difficult. It can seem nonspiritual, overly intellectual. Some passages will require repeated reading and careful thought. But the Holy Spirit, who first inspired the words in Scripture, now illumines our hearts to receive and understand them. He's eager to open our eyes to see wonderful things in God's Word (Ps. 119:18).

But we don't have to do this alone. The Spirit has gifted the church with individuals who can help us understand Scripture better, beginning with your pastor. We can also take advantage of commentaries, study Bibles, and books.[9] The best ones explain what a passage says in its literary, historical, and redemptive context and lead us to value Scripture more highly. The worst offer opinions or sow doubts. In commenting on the wisdom and necessity of reading other books, Charles Spurgeon succinctly said, "He who will not use the thoughts of other men's brains, proves that he has no brains of his own."[10]

When we take time to read and reflect upon God as the object of our worship, we're expending energy toward having a real knowledge of the most glorious and valuable being in the universe. That knowledge is a gift from God that enables us to love him more passionately, obey him more consistently, serve him more joyfully, and trust him more confidently. It's what enables us to be numbered among the worshipers of God.

ALWAYS RECEIVERS

Our first responsibility as worshipers is to understand what God has given us in Jesus Christ and the Holy Spirit. Refusing to come to God by grace or seeking to know him apart from the Bible moves us away from God, not toward him. In fact, God gives us his Spirit so we "might understand the things freely given us by God" (1 Cor. 2:12). Left on our own we'd never begin to imagine how gracious and good God is. If you thought worship was all about you, this is good news. Incredible news.

God has removed every hindrance to having a relationship with him. If we come by his grace, there is nothing that need stand in the way of our worshiping him. Nothing.

One of the most specific references to God's invitation to us to draw near is found in the book of Hebrews. After explaining how inadequate the Old Testament priests and sacrifices were to fully and permanently open the way to God, the author says this:

> Therefore, brothers, since we have confidence to enter the holy places by the blood of Jesus, by the new and living way that he opened for us through the curtain, that is, through his flesh, and since we have a great priest over the house of God, let us draw near with a true heart in full assurance of faith, with our hearts sprinkled clean from an evil conscience and our bodies washed with pure water. (Heb. 10:19–22)

After centuries of God warning his people not to draw close without the proper sacrifices, God now cries out through the blood of Jesus, his Son, "Come near!" His once-for-all sacrifice has thrown open the door to the throne room of God. We come at God's invitation and by God's enabling. We come to marvel at his grace, stand in awe of his holiness, and be undone by his mercy. We come to gaze upon his beauty, drink in his promises, and embrace his will for our lives.

Through Jesus, and Jesus alone, we now have free access by the Spirit into the Father's presence.

There is nothing left to do but receive, rejoice, and worship.

3

TRUE WORSHIPERS *EXALT*

WORSHIP AND HUMILITY

> I will bless the LORD at all times;
> his praise shall continually be in my mouth.
> My soul makes its boast in the LORD;
> let the humble hear and be glad.
> Oh, magnify the LORD with me,
> and let us exalt his name together!
>
> PSALM 34:1–3

We were two years into a church plant in the nineties and experiencing typical church-planting challenges. Some individuals who were with us from the start decided to join another church. A few disgruntled parents didn't like our parent-driven youth ministry. A man who had been caught in sexual immorality accused me of insensitive counseling.

God used these situations and others to expose how much I wanted to look good in the eyes of others. And it was ugly. So in early January of 1994 I wrote this brief prayer in my journal: "God, do whatever you need to do to deal with the pride in my life."

He did.

A few weeks later, while I was at a friend's house for dinner, a wave of sheer panic gripped me out of nowhere. In an instant, I felt cut off from my past, my future, and everyone in the room. I was tempted to collapse in a fetal position but managed to excuse myself from the table. After locking myself in the bathroom, I started praying. Feverishly. *God, what is happening? What is this? Where are you?*

Silence.

That night I began a journey of almost three years battling depression, anxiety, disconnectedness, tension, and a profound, incessant hopelessness. A physical exam showed I was fine, and I had no external crises.

After much prayer, counsel, Bible study, and reflection, I discovered the root of my problem.

Worship.

WORSHIP IN THE WRONG DIRECTION

It wasn't a lack of worship that caused my breakdown. It was worship in the wrong direction.

Worship in the wrong direction is called idolatry. It's looking to anything other than God for our ultimate satisfaction, comfort, security, or joy. When I worship an idol, I'm saying, "Fulfill me. Console me. Protect me. Rule me. You are worthy of my strength, time, energy, and affections. Only you can make me completely happy." We don't physically bow down to our idols. But that's what we're doing in our hearts.

I was living proof that "we never begin worship; we aim it."[1] We're always worshiping something, someone. I had been aiming at the idols of control and reputation for years, and God finally allowed me to experience the effects. Instead of trusting in God's sovereignty, I sought refuge in my own ability to control things. Instead of magnifying God's mercy, I was promoting my own efforts to earn his favor. Instead of exalting God, I exalted me. And when I couldn't get the glory I craved, my world came crashing down.

Over time God helped me see that when I sought glory for myself, praise for my accomplishments, and credit for my growth, I wasn't exalting a Savior—I was searching for an audience. Thankfully, Jesus died for that as well.

Through a lengthy and painful process, God redirected my worship. I came to see in a fresh and profound way that we're redeemed to exalt God and God alone.

WORDS OF WORSHIP

It's significant that in Scripture the Hebrew and Greek words we most often translate as "worship" originally expressed the custom of bowing down or casting oneself on the ground.[2] Other "worship" words in the Bible convey a variety of attitudes and activities that include submission, sacrifice, serving, and even fear.[3] They cover what we do, not only in our meetings but also in our daily lives. They speak to our words and actions as well as our minds and hearts.

That's why *exalt* seems to be an appropriate word to sum up how God calls true worshipers to respond to him. To worship God is to humble everything about ourselves and exalt everything about him. It's to acknowledge that he alone is exalted over all peoples, all gods, and all the heavens (Pss. 99:2; 97:9; 108:5). It's to rejoice in the reality that he is "exalted as head above all" (1 Chron. 29:11).

In Scripture, every description of our relationship with God communicates the relationship of a lesser to a greater. We're creatures of the Creator (Rev. 4:11), servants of the Master (Luke 17:10), children of the Father (1 John 3:1), the bride of the Bridegroom (Rev. 19:7), the house of the Builder (Heb. 3:6), the branches of the Vine (John 15:5). When God calls us friends, it only highlights his extraordinary condescension and mercy toward us (John 15:15; James 2:23).

Even as a Christian I had been contending with God for worship. But God is jealous for his glory and loves us enough to change us. So his Spirit mercifully opened my eyes to see what I had missed: God is God and I am not.

Happily, God is always reminding true worshipers there's someone greater than themselves to exalt.

WHAT DOES EXALTING GOD LOOK LIKE?

A popular worship song from the seventies that's still sung today includes the chorus,

> I exalt Thee, I exalt Thee,
> I exalt Thee, O Lord!

I remember singing it over and over and being moved by the devotion it expressed. But we're deceived if we think *singing* is necessarily the same as *doing*. That would be like saying, "I hug you," as I pass by my wife, thinking my words are a sufficient replacement for actual physical contact. My words are meaningless without actions to back them up.

God intends us to exalt him not only with our songs but also with our lives. In Paul's letter to the Romans, after explaining and exulting in the gospel for eleven chapters, he makes this plea: "I appeal to you therefore, brothers, by the mercies of God, to present your bodies as a living sacrifice, holy and acceptable to God, which is your spiritual worship" (Rom. 12:1). Paul's use of the word *bodies* is intentional. In response to God's mercy, we're to worship God not simply with our words, feelings, or momentary acts—but also with our bodies, our lives. Worship offered to God can't be confined to what we do in a room on Sunday morning. It's more than simply lifting our hands or having a transcendent emotional experience. Our worship includes the ordinary and mundane things we think, say, and do each day, as well as the more significant and spectacular. It's an all-of-life response to the forgiveness we've received through the gospel.

To sum up what we've seen thus far, *true worshipers, enabled and redeemed by God, respond to God's self-revelation in ways that exalt his glory in Christ in their minds, affections, and wills, by the power of the Holy Spirit.* God calls us to magnify his greatness and goodness to us through Jesus in every way possible, internally and externally. Worship begins in our hearts but always works its way out into visible actions. Here are some ways we can exalt God with both.

EXALTING GOD IN OUR HEARTS

These lists aren't meant to be comprehensive. But I hope they serve as a springboard for considering the rich and varied ways we can glorify God as true worshipers.

Through Our Thoughts

The first and most basic way we exalt God is simply by remembering he exists! "The fool says in his heart, 'There is no God'" (Ps. 14:1). In contrast, true worshipers realize God is always aware, always involved, always working for our good and for his glory.

We can exalt the Lord at any moment simply by asking, Where is God in this picture? Your picture might be painful. A car breaking down. A spouse leaving. An unexpected bill arriving in the mail. Hearing that the child you're expecting has a physical abnormality. Finding it impossible to talk to your parents or children. Being let go by your employer. In each of these situations we have the choice of forgetting God or remembering that he is present and active. Turning our thoughts to God highlights the truth that "in him we live and move and have our being" (Acts 17:28).

It's difficult to imagine Job's anguish when he learned he had lost all his possessions and children. But as he fell down and worshiped, his first thoughts were about God. "The LORD gave, and the LORD has taken away; blessed be the name of the LORD" (Job 1:21). Job went on to endure ongoing physical agony and inaccurate counsel from his friends. He questioned God, argued with God, and got angry at God. But he never stopped thinking about God. That's because for Job, God was always in the picture, even if Job didn't understand what he was up to.[4]

One believer from a few centuries ago prayed these words as he considered his tendency to forget God: "I confess that You have not been in all my thoughts, that the knowledge of Yourself as the end of my being has been strangely overlooked, that I have never seriously considered my heart-need."[5]

Our heart need is to remember that God is the great "I AM," the unshakeable, unchanging, ever-present reality. If it's true, as Paul says, that "from him and through him and to him are all things" (Rom. 11:36), then there's something about our present circumstances that involves God. Whatever our situation happens to be, God is the most important participant.

Through Our Love

True worshipers do more than think about God. They love him. Jesus said that the greatest commandment is this: "You shall love the Lord your God with all your heart and with all your soul and with all your mind and with all your strength" (Mark 12:30).

Because worship and love are so closely connected, whatever we love most will determine what we genuinely worship. Love speaks of the desires and motives behind our relationship with God. While love is more than feelings, it's not less than feelings. It speaks of wanting, enjoying, and treasuring Christ, not simply following rules, memorizing Bible verses, and going to church meetings. Loving God turns duty into delight, perfunctory obedience into passionate pursuit, stoic endurance into faith-filled hope.

It should be evident how loving God exalts him. When we love something, we attach worth to it. We're saying to others, "*This* is worthy of my thoughts, time, labors, and affections." Loving God persuades others that God is desirable, good, and satisfying. Loving God is distinct from loving things *about* God. It's the difference between Bible knowledge that leads to pride and that which leads to praise.

People who exalt God by loving him are the ones who look forward to spending time in God's Word because of the opportunity to hear his voice. They get more excited about introducing someone to Christ than about meeting somebody famous. They're often affected when they hear testimonies of God's goodness and faithfulness. Conversations with them regularly end up at the foot of the cross, thanking God for his mercy. Knowing them makes you want to know the Savior better.

And that exalts him.

But Jesus didn't stop at commanding us to love God. He went on to say, "You shall love your neighbor as yourself" (Mark 12:31). It brings no glory to God if we claim deep affection for God while harboring ill will toward people. In fact, John says that's an impossible situation: "He who does not love his brother whom he has seen cannot love God whom he has not seen" (1 John 4:20). Loving others, even when they're unlovable, exalts God because it reflects his heart toward us. It tells others we're his children. We're acting like our heavenly Father, who "makes his sun rise on the evil and on the good, and sends rain on the just and on the unjust" (Matt. 5:45). Loving others points to the humility, compassion, gentleness, and patience the Savior has shown us (Eph. 4:1–2; 5:2).

And that exalts God, too.

Through Our Faith

Faith is not only the doorway into the Christian life but our ongoing expression of trust in God. The purpose of faith isn't to secure wealth and health in the here and now but to remind ourselves that in Jesus Christ, God has already given us everything (1 Cor. 3:21–23: Eph. 1:3). Faith reaches out to God with open hands, believing that he will fill them because of his character and promises. "Without faith it is impossible to please him, for whoever would draw near to God must believe that he exists and that he rewards those who seek him" (Heb. 11:6).

Exercising faith toward God puts his wisdom on display. Instead of trusting worldly perspectives or our own ideas of how things should be done, we're acknowledging that God knows all things, and we don't (Prov. 3:5).

Exercising faith toward God puts his power on display. Though our strength is inadequate, our supplies insufficient, and our efforts ineffective, we join Job in saying,

> I know that you can do all things,
>> and that no purpose of yours can be thwarted. (Job 42:2)

Exercising faith toward God puts his faithfulness on display. When we're not sure how we're going to pay for unexpected medical bills, our trust in God exalts his promise to care and provide for us (1 Pet. 5:7). We're proclaiming to others that God's promise is true: "I will never leave you nor forsake you" (Heb. 13:5).

Simply rehearsing our problems doesn't exalt God; recalling his character in the midst of them does. We see that in Psalms 42 and 43. The writer feels far from God and is being persecuted by his enemies. Rather than simply complain, he reminds himself three times that God is his hope and salvation:

> Why are you cast down, O my soul,
>> and why are you in turmoil within me?
> Hope in God; for I shall again praise him,
>> my salvation and my God. (Pss. 42:5–6, 11; 43:5)

Success, fruitfulness, and a trouble-free life aren't the only ways God glorifies himself through us. Even in the midst of our suffering we can exalt him as we trust his power to sustain, comfort, and deliver.

> Trust in him at all times, O people;
>> pour out your heart before him;
>> God is a refuge for us. (Ps. 62:8)

Through Our Gratefulness

God commands us over and over to give him thanks.[6] Have you ever wondered why? God isn't encouraging us to be polite, as a mother would urge her four-year-old, "Ricky, remember to thank your Aunt Marge for your birthday present." No, God is rooting our hearts in reality. "Every good gift and every perfect gift is from above, coming down from the Father of lights with whom there is no variation or shadow due to change" (James 1:17). He has blessed us more than we could ask or imagine, and our gratefulness, usually expressed in words of thanks, points people to the source of our blessings.

A grateful heart highlights God's lavish grace and kindness toward us. God is constantly showering us with good gifts, some of which are more obvious (health, food, clothing, family, friends), and many of which aren't (air we can breathe, protection from accidents that never happened, prayers of others, good works that we have yet to walk in).

In contrast, an ungrateful heart casts suspicion on God's character and dishonors him. Our attitude communicates that God isn't aware of our situation, doesn't care about us enough to be involved, or isn't powerful enough to do anything. It comes as no surprise that a primary root of unbelief is a refusal to thank God (Rom. 1:21).

Above all, true worshipers always have reason for astonished thankfulness because their names are written in the Lamb's Book of Life. We have no fear of coming judgment. Our sins have been paid for through the once-for-all death of Christ at Calvary. God is our Father and will be for endless ages. That's why more than once the psalmists bring glory to God by declaring, "I will give thanks to you *forever*" (Ps. 30:12; cf. Pss. 44:8; 52:9; 79:13).

Through Our Longing

We live in the age of "the already and the not yet."[7] Jesus has risen from the dead, but people still die. The Devil is defeated, but he still seems to have free rein on earth. Jesus has come, but we yearn for his coming again, when he'll make all things right.

But today, they're not all right. Some people battle chronic, almost unbearable pain. A young mother is devastated by the sudden death of her five-month-old. A father of seven young children inexplicably dies while jumping on a trampoline. Breathtaking advances in modern medicine aren't enough to prevent people from losing their lives to cancer, AIDS, heart disease, and strokes. The grave yawns wide before us. Thousands of social media campaigns and billions of pledged dollars in aid barely scratch the surface in the fight against disease and poverty. Marriages end in divorce. Children are abducted, raped, and sold into sex slavery. Creation groans.

We can identify with the repeated cry of Scripture, "How long, O LORD?" (Ps. 13:1; cf. Ps. 90:13; Rev. 6:10). And in that cry we're expressing our confidence in God's sovereignty, his justice, his love for his church and creation, and his faithfulness to his promises.

Ultimately, true worshipers know all their longings for God will be fulfilled when the Savior returns and we see "our blessed hope, the appearing of the glory of our great God and Savior, Jesus Christ" (Titus 2:13). We stake our lives on the fact that "according to his promise we are waiting for new heavens and a new earth in which righteousness dwells" (2 Pet. 3:13).

We aren't putting our hope in a pipe dream. Nor are we kept from seeking to right the wrongs we see now. We just know that the day of his return will come.

And we exalt God by continually longing for it.

EXALTING GOD IN OUR ACTIONS

Exalting God on the inside is accompanied by visible evidences on the outside. Those evidences involve "spiritual" activities such as praying, reading our Bibles, and singing, but they go beyond that. *Everything* we do can be done to exalt

God's greatness and goodness in Jesus Christ. "So, whether you eat or drink, or whatever you do, do *all* to the glory of God" (1 Cor. 10:31).

Here are just a few of the ways we can worship God through the things we do.

Through Our Willing Obedience

Obeying God isn't legalism, nor is it optional. The idea that someone can be a true worshiper and be unconcerned about obedience is foreign to Scripture. Jesus said it clearly: "If you love me, you will keep my commandments" (John 14:15).

Our obedience doesn't earn us a place in God's kingdom but shows that God has brought us into his kingdom through the atoning work of Christ. The fact that all our sins have been paid for only makes us more eager to reflect the character of the One who saved us and said, "You shall be holy, for I am holy" (1 Pet. 1:14–16).

Submitting to God's commands tells others that we love him and that his laws are good and worthy to be followed. We make it evident that God is the King, that we are not, and that he deserves our allegiance. And in all our obedience we proclaim that serving God is true freedom, not bondage (Gal. 5:13).

Obedience is often fleshed out in specific relationships. In Paul's letters to the Ephesians and Colossians, and in Peter's first letter, various groups of people are addressed—husbands, wives, parents, children, employers, and employees (Eph. 5:22–6:9; Col. 3:18–4:1; 1 Pet. 2:18–3:7). Each group is given specific ways they're to please the Lord. Husbands are to love their wives as their own bodies and live with them in an understanding way. Wives are to submit to and respect their husbands. Children are to obey their parents, while parents are to raise their children in the discipline and instruction of the Lord. Employers are to be just and fair, while employees are to serve their employers diligently. As related groups obey God in complementary ways, they exalt the wisdom of God's design and order.

But there are also ways by which every Christian can bring glory to God. Joyfully pursuing purity shows that God's love is more gratifying than fleeting sensual pleasure. Exercising moderation in eating glorifies God by responding to his gifts with gratefulness rather than greed. Keeping our anger in check points to the One who has been infinitely patient with us. Caring for those less fortunate exalts the Savior who "though he was rich, yet for your sake . . . became poor, so that you by his poverty might become rich" (2 Cor. 8:9).

While we will never follow God's commands completely or perfectly in this life, our obedience makes a public statement of their truth, value, and sweetness (Ps. 19:7–10).

Through Our Specific Praise

The psalmist says,

> The heavens declare the glory of God,
> and the sky above proclaims his handiwork. (Ps. 19:1)

Whether or not we proclaim God's greatness, creation always will.

But creation's praise is voiceless and limited in how much it can communicate. God has given human beings the particular privilege of giving him specific, intelligent praise. When a new baby arrives, or we marvel at the star-clustered night sky, or a friend gets a promotion, it exalts God to let others know he is the one ultimately responsible. He is the source of our joy and delight and deserves to be honored. Responding occasionally with, "Praise the Lord!" or "Thank God!" might sound like a cliché, but it can be an improvement on the more typical "Awesome!" or "Cool!"

Rarely does Scripture exhort us to praise the Lord without spelling out why.

> Praise the Lord!
> Oh give thanks to the Lord, for he is good,
> > for his steadfast love endures forever! (Ps. 106:1)

> Praise the Lord!
> Blessed is the man who fears the Lord,
> > who greatly delights in his commandments! (Ps. 112:1)

> Praise the Lord!
> Praise God in his sanctuary;
> > praise him in his mighty heavens!
> Praise him for his mighty deeds;
> > praise him according to his excellent greatness!
> > > (Ps. 150:1–2)

The Psalms are filled with examples of God's people declaring in particular ways what God has revealed about himself. Specifically, they praise God for his Word, his worthiness, and his works (Pss. 56:4; 105:2; 145:8–9).[8] Those categories can serve us as we seek to expand our own vocabulary of worship.

It's true that God is great. But we can thank him specifically for giving us his Word so we can know his plans, desires, and promises. And yes, God is awesome. But we can marvel, in particular, that he spoke the universe into existence with a word. God is powerful. But we can ponder that he controls the courses of planets and the paths of arrows (1 Kings 22:29–38). And God certainly is holy. But that means he is infinitely exalted above his creation and absolutely separate from moral impurity. Yes, God is glorious. But we see his glory in all its perfection when we consider the Son of God hanging in the place of sinful rebels, displaying God's justice, righteousness, compassion, wisdom, power, and love.

You get the idea. God has given Christians alone the opportunity to exalt him through specific, gospel-grateful praise. True worshipers don't want to miss out on it.

Through Our Godly Speech

Every time we open our mouths we're speaking words of worship. As Jesus told the Pharisees, "Out of the abundance of the heart the mouth speaks" (Matt. 12:34). Since our hearts are always exalting something, it follows that our words reflect what our hearts are worshiping at any given moment.

Words of encouragement exalt God by pointing out the ways he has been at work in the lives of others. Truthful words bring glory to the God who cannot lie. Confessing sin is a sign that we agree with God's assessment of us and an expression of gratefulness that our sins have been forgiven in Christ.

In contrast, when I yell at my kids in anger for interrupting me while I'm watching TV, I'm exalting my convenience over God's command to be gentle (Titus 3:2). When I engage in criticism, gossip, and slander, I'm not only exalting myself over others but also grieving God's Holy Spirit (Eph. 4:29–30). When I participate in sexually provocative conversation, I'm exalting my desire for sensual titillation over God's command to be grateful and holy (Eph. 5:4; 1 Thess. 4:7). Complaining and comparison show that I think more highly of my wants than of God's commands to be content (1 Tim. 6:8; Heb. 13:5). Every word we say is worship.

Our words are not our own—even when we share them on blogs, Facebook, Twitter, or texts. They were given to us to draw attention to the living Word, without whom we would have no words at all.

Through Our Grace-Motivated Serving

Serving rooted in grace exalts God because it communicates that there is greater joy in serving others than in being self-centered, that no one has served us like Jesus has, and that there's no one more worthy of being served than Jesus himself.

Our serving doesn't automatically bring glory to God. We can serve with bad attitudes, with impatient hearts, out of expediency, or to impress others. But true worshipers are first of all receivers who know that their serving originates not in themselves, but in God's good gifts. Considering how God enables us to serve transforms our service into Christ-exalting worship.

God gives us abilities with which to serve. "As each has received a gift, use it to serve one another, as good stewards of God's varied grace" (1 Pet. 4:10). The fact that *each* has received a gift means we're never consigned to being mere spectators. God wants to display the beauty of his grace through every one of his children.

God gives us the desire to serve. "For it is God who works in you, both to will and to work for his good pleasure" (Phil. 2:13). When we know our motivation comes from God, our serving will be characterized by joy and faithfulness, even when the task is unpleasant or inconvenient. We'll view taking out the trash, changing a diaper, or visiting a sick friend as more of a privilege than a pain.

God gives us the strength to serve. Paul evaluated his ministry at one point by saying, "I worked harder than any of them, though it was not I, but the grace of God that is with me" (1 Cor. 15:10). Paul's zealous serving brought glory to God because he knew the strength wasn't his own. He refused to take credit for it.

In Jesus, God gives us the supreme example of serving. Though he was God, he "did not count equality with God a thing to be grasped, but emptied himself, by taking the form of a servant, being born in the likeness of men. And being found in human form, he humbled himself by becoming obedient to the point of death, even death on a cross" (Phil. 2:6–8). Jesus demonstrates servanthood in making us his bride (Rev. 21:9), washing our feet (John 13:3–5), calling us friends (John 15:15), and welcoming us as his brothers and sisters (Rom. 8:29).[9] But he hasn't just served us. He has saved us. And that makes us all the more eager to serve others.

Through Our Faithful Witness

One of the first things the woman at the well wanted to do was go back to town to tell her friends about Jesus. It's what we always want to do when we've discovered something truly remarkable. The only difference is that for Christians, someone truly remarkable has "discovered" *us*—and we have a hard time keeping the news to ourselves.

I've known individuals who are fairly tight-lipped in normal conversations. But mention their favorite sport, TV show, hobby, or band, and they light up. Their words flow, right along with their passion. We talk about what has touched us most deeply. That's why there's no strict divide between evangelism and worship. Evangelism, or telling others the good news of the gospel, is simply praising God in front of those who don't know him.

> I will give thanks to you, O Lord, among the peoples;
> I will sing praises to you among the nations. (Ps. 57:9)

God never intended us to exalt him on Sunday morning with other Christians and remain quiet about him the rest of the week. True worshipers, like the Samaritan woman, can't hold it in. "Come, see a man who told me all that I ever did" (John 4:29).

NEVER MOVING ON FROM THE GOSPEL

We have no power in and of ourselves to do the things I just listed, much less all the things I *didn't* mention. We might wake up every day for the rest of our lives intending to exalt God in all these ways—and fail. Our prayers will be stained with selfish motives, our obedience will be incomplete, and our sins will be many. We will do things we shouldn't do and leave undone things we should do.

But just as we weren't the beginning of the story, we aren't the end of it either. When God invites and enables us to exalt him, he doesn't then leave us on our own. He points us to Jesus who perfectly fulfilled his commands. Because we need God to worship God.

This doesn't mean the gospel is opposed to hard work. True worshipers seek to exalt God with all their heart, soul, mind, and strength. We "make every effort" to grow in Christian virtue and be fruitful for God's glory (2 Pet. 1:5–8). But our labors don't earn us a place in God's family. They're a sign that God has brought us in through the gospel. We pursue exalting God because we've received the indescribable gift of salvation.

The gospel is the greatest encouragement we could ever hope to have as we seek to exalt God through our lives. Jesus lived the life of perfect obedience we could never live, and that life is now credited to us. He endured God's wrath as our substitute to reconcile us to God. The Father raised Jesus from the dead to prove that his payment for our sins was accepted and to assure us that one day we too will be raised from death to life.

When we fail, the gospel reminds us we're forgiven. When we glorify God willingly, the gospel reminds us to be grateful. We're simply carrying out the good works God planned for us to do before we were even born (Eph. 2:10).

In every way and at every moment, the gospel enables us to exalt God's great name. And as we'll see in the next chapter, he intends for us to do that not only as individuals, but together.

TRUE WORSHIPERS *GATHER*

WORSHIP AND COMMUNITY

... not neglecting to meet together, as is the habit of some, but encouraging one another, and all the more as you see the Day drawing near.

HEBREWS 10:25

It's 9:08 on Sunday morning, and Steve and Sandy are rushing madly to get their three kids out the door in time for the Sunday service. The drive is just over fifteen minutes. If all the lights are green. On this particular morning all but one are red.

Slightly irritated, Steve pulls into a parking space on the far side of the lot at 9:28, and scrambles to get to the building. As they walk through the doors they hear the congregation singing but have to check their little ones into Kids' Church first.

They finally make it to the service and settle into the back row. As the third song finishes, the pastor steps up to pray and receive the offering. He makes a few announcements, introduces a special song, and then continues his series from the book of Philippians. Steve is trying to stay focused, but it's not working. His thoughts keep drifting to this afternoon when a couple of the guys are coming over to watch the game. Sandy's wondering whether she has enough snacks to feed them. After a closing song, Steve and Sandy are on the move again. They pick up their kids and hurry home for a quick lunch so their two youngest can get their naps.

This scenario, or something like it, is repeated hundreds of thousands of times each week. Maybe you can relate. I know I can. Sunday mornings become just one more activity to fit into your already packed and overwhelming schedule.

Wouldn't it be easier just to stay home? After all, Christians can read the Bible and exalt God all by themselves—on their own, with no one near them. Isn't that what true worshipers do Monday through Saturday?

But then Sunday comes around. Every week. And if we're honest, there are probably weeks we wish Sunday didn't come. It means getting out of bed early to spend an hour or two with people we don't know very well, some of whom we'd rather not know at all. There are always things to critique about our church, and if you're a parent with young kids, or a student who stayed up late Saturday night with friends, or a businessman who's been out of town all week, the reasons to "do church on your own" can sound *very* compelling.

But true worshipers gather. They understand the heart of the psalmist when he says,

Praise the LORD!
I will give thanks to the LORD with my whole heart,
   in the company of the upright, in the congregation.
    (Ps. 111:1)

Thanking and praising God in the midst of the congregation is more than a good idea. It's what true worshipers were made for and central to what God is doing on the earth.

It's possible we've lost sight of the history as well as the benefits of meeting together. Let's look at both.

A GATHERED PEOPLE

From the first, God wanted a people who would declare the greatness of his name through the words and witness of their life together. "Even in earliest times," says pastor and professor Iain Duguid, "worship is not a solitary event but a communal event. Both Adam and Eve are made in God's image, created to be his representatives on earth, doing him homage, worshiping and serving him together."[1]

Adam and Eve were a type of the community God would eventually redeem for himself from all the nations on the earth. God never intended our worship to be just "me and God." That's because our worship is the outflow of the relationships the Father, Son, and Spirit have always enjoyed.

God isn't a solitary God. There is only one God, but he has existed as three persons from all eternity. The Father, Son, and Holy Spirit have always experienced triune joy, giving and taking, sharing together a depth of relationship and love that human relationships are meant to echo. In his kindness,

God saves us so we might experience the same joys of fellowship, outpouring, and mutual love he does.

God says (in Gen. 2:18), "It is not good that the man should be alone." This is a statement not only of our need for relationship, but also of God's desire to have his glory expressed in community. God never intended us to live in isolation from each other.

At Mount Sinai, God calls the Israelites "a kingdom of priests and a holy nation" (Ex. 19:6). While God expected individual and family devotion to him, the Israelite year was marked by annual festivals where God's people gathered to celebrate his goodness and renew his covenant with them.

In the New Testament, this corporate image is even clearer. Paul declares that the church is "the temple of the living God" (2 Cor. 6:16). Elsewhere he refers to us as "God's field, God's building" (1 Cor. 3:9). In Ephesians 2, he calls the church a household with foundations and a cornerstone, a structure joined together to be a holy temple in whom God dwells (Eph. 2:19–21). Peter echoes the book of Exodus when he describes the church as "a chosen race, a royal priesthood, a holy nation, a people for [God's] own possession" (1 Pet. 2:9). These passages drive home the significance God places on the church meeting and living out life *together*.

We see that fleshed out in the pages of the New Testament. The early church breaks bread together, prays together, learns together, shares resources together, suffers together, attends the temple together, and shares the gospel together (Acts 2:42, 46; 4:32; 5:41–42).

Bottom line: God doesn't give us a choice about whether we want to be in the church. If we're Christians, we're already part of the family. The question then becomes where and how we work out the details of family life.

BENEFITS OF THE WORSHIPING COMMUNITY

Scripture and church history affirm that certain activities will be part of almost every church gathering. We sing, pray, give offerings, confess our faith, greet one another, teach and admonish each other, exercise spiritual gifts, hear God's Word proclaimed and taught, participate in the sacraments, and more.

While we could do many of these things alone, we receive greater benefit as we do them together. Here are a few reasons why.

Remembering and Rehearsing the Gospel

Robert Robinson confessed in his famous hymn "Come Thou Fount of Every Blessing" that he was "prone to wander." There's nothing we're more prone to wander from than our reliance on the gospel. And we tend to wander more quickly when we neglect to meet with the church.

In his excellent book *Christ-Centered Worship*, Bryan Chapell writes, "Corporate worship is nothing more, and nothing less, than a representation of the gospel in the presence of God and his people for his glory and their good."[2] We meet together as redeemed saints to remind each other whose we are, how we got here, and why it matters.

Remembering and rehearsing God's saving acts is a practice rooted in the Old Testament. There, particularly in the Psalms, we read repeatedly about God delivering his people from the bondage of Egypt.[3] In the New Testament, we celebrate God's greater deliverance through Christ from our bondage to sin. Jesus gave us the Lord's Supper as an ongoing way to remember his death when we meet (1 Cor. 11:23–26). Paul says we're to let the "word of Christ"—the gospel— dwell in us richly as we sing (Col. 3:16). He reminds the Corinthians that the gospel is of first importance (1 Cor. 15:1–4). In both the Old and New Testaments, God gathers his people so that we won't forget our relationship with him or what he did to establish it.

If you're part of a church that follows a historic liturgy each week, you can probably recognize a progression that begins with the adoration of God, confession of our sin, and assurance of our forgiveness through the substitutionary death of Christ. That's meant to remind us of the gospel. Since the earliest days of the church, liturgies have been designed to teach and protect gospel truths. While liturgies vary in details and can be performed mindlessly, they're meant to reflect a structure that outlines the story of the gospel and our response to it.

Gathering to rehearse and remember the gospel addresses our common temptations. We struggle under the weight of condemnation. We wonder if God loves us. We're puffed up with pride at how well we're doing. We lose sight of God's holiness and what it cost to forgive us.

The gospel speaks to all those situations and more. Jesus Christ has paid for all our sins. We can never be separated from God's love in Christ. Our only boast is the cross of Christ—not our accomplishments (Rom. 8:38–39; Gal. 6:14; Eph. 1:7). The gospel is an endless source of encouragement, strength, comfort, and motivation for weary souls. That's why we gather to remember it.

Receiving God's Word Together

Throughout Scripture, God gathered his people to address them through his Word (Ex. 19:7; 2 Kings 23:1–3; Neh. 8:1). Preaching formed a central part of early church gatherings as God-ordained pastors and teachers sought to nurture and equip believers under their care (Acts 20:28; Eph. 4:11–12; 2 Tim. 4:2).

In 1 Timothy 5, Paul speaks of the pastors "who labor in preaching and teaching" (5:17). While all elders must be able to teach (3:2), God gifts certain ones to lead, guide, guard, and feed God's people through proclaiming his Word in the context of the gathered church. They're not motivational speakers giving inspiring talks. They're equipping the saints for works of ministry, and one day they'll give an account to God for those they're preaching to (Eph. 4:11–12; Heb. 13:17). If we never gather to sit under their preaching, how will they give an account for us?

When the church gathers expectantly in one place at one time to hear God's Word proclaimed, it's a unique event. God himself addresses us as his people. The Spirit works in our hearts at once to convict, comfort, illumine, and exhort. Not only are we being strengthened individually; we're being strengthened as a body.

It's God's kindness that we're able to download sermons we missed or messages from churches we don't even attend. But neither of those possibilities contributes as directly to strengthening our unity as sitting under the preaching of God's Word together. We can thank God for opportunities to listen to messages on our own. We can thank him even more that we get to hear them with the church.

Mutual Serving and Caring

Each Sunday I marvel at the variety of ways I'm served by the people in my church. Some arrive early to set up equipment. Others joyfully greet guests at the door. Some serve by receiving the offering and distributing communion. A few women faithfully serve moms with nursing babies. We have children's ministry teachers, vocalists, tech personnel, videographers, projectionists, instrumentalists, welcome-center hosts, van drivers, and more. I walk away encouraged by their example every week.

That's exactly what's supposed to happen. The writer of Hebrews tells us we gather "to stir up one another to love and good works" (Heb. 10:24). I'm stirred up as I benefit from the different strengths, gifts, and abilities God has given to other members of my church. I need to be stirred up regularly. So do you.

Every Christian has been gifted in some way to serve his or her local church (1 Cor. 12:4–7; 1 Pet. 4:10). Of course that serving can and should take place outside Sunday mornings. But when we don't meet together, we limit the opportunities we have to serve each other.

Our corporate gatherings provide an abundance of occasions, both planned and spontaneous, for receiving and expressing the grace of God we enjoy through the gospel.

A Greater Awareness of God's Presence

In Scripture God chooses certain times and places to reveal his presence in pronounced and unique ways. One of those times is when the church gathers.

We don't have to scour the Internet to locate the latest outpouring of the Spirit. We don't have to chase experiences and manifestations of the Holy Spirit "out there"—because he's already promised to be "right here" as we meet with our local church.

Iain Duguid writes:

> Why can't we worship just as well in front of the TV set, where the music and the preaching may well be more inspiring? The reason is that as the covenant community together we are the new temple. . . . There is something about corporate worship which is not present in individual worship, and that "something" is a fuller expression of the reality of God's presence.[4]

I might experience a fuller expression of the reality of God's presence as we're singing "It is well with my soul" and a fresh awareness of God's care and sovereignty fills me. As the pastor is preaching I might be convicted of sin in a particular area. As someone prays, my heart might rise up with Spirit-inspired faith for a difficult situation I'm facing. As we celebrate the Lord's Supper, I might be overwhelmed with joy that all my sins have been paid for through the blood of Christ. All this is "normal" for the gathered church because as the new temple in Jesus Christ, the church is where God's presence is now typically encountered.

Demonstrating Our Unity in the Gospel

The scattered church throughout the week is still the church. But gathering together is a physical demonstration and reminder of our distinctness from the world and our unity in the gospel. We show that we've been drawn apart from the world and drawn together to God.

Being one in Christ is more than meeting regularly in the same room, but it isn't less. Singing songs, reciting creeds, and reading Scripture together are ways of declaring to myself and others that I'm part of a holy temple, not just a random brick or a loose stone (Eph. 2:19–22). "Christian proclamation might make the gospel audible," writes pastor and theologian Mark Dever, "but Christians living together in local congregations make the gospel visible (see John 13:34–35)."[5]

That's one thing that distinguishes the local church from attending conferences or large Christian gatherings. While God can work in our lives through those events, they lack the advantage of ongoing pastoral oversight. Conferees haven't lived *life* together or worked out the details of doctrinal differences. The sense of oneness can be a temporary unity or, even worse, a deceptive unity.

Most of us instinctively (sinfully?) like to be with people who are a lot like us—people who like the same music, eat at the same restaurants, and shop at the same stores. But God is glorified when people who have no visible connection or similarity joyfully meet together week after week. They do it not because they're all the same but because the gospel has brought them together.

Bitter believers sometimes comment that they find more fellowship on Saturday nights at the bar than Sunday mornings at their church. The right response isn't to hang out more at the bar but to *become* the kind of church that expresses the love, power, encouragement, and unity we find only in the gospel. True worshipers desire to exalt God's name *together* (Ps. 34:3).

Sharing the Sacraments

Another way the unifying power of the gospel is made visible when we gather is through the sacraments of baptism and the Lord's Supper. When people are baptized, they're publicly identifying with Christ's death, burial, and resurrection. But expressing their union with Christ is paramount to expressing their union with the church. No one is baptized into Christ who isn't also baptized into his body.

That's why it's most appropriate for a pastor of a church to baptize new believers and for other members of the congregation to be present. It's a celebration of how God has added a new member to the household of faith. Since the church is the physical representation of Christ's presence on earth, baptism is typically the doorway into the household.

In a similar way, sharing communion signifies and confirms our unity as a body and is an act of worship that brings glory to God. It's also a unique moment when, through faith, we experience together in a fresh way our union with Christ. Paul says to the Corinthians, "The cup of blessing that we bless, is it not a participation in the blood of Christ? The bread that we break, is it not a participation in the body of Christ? Because there is one bread, we who are many are one body, for we all partake of the one bread" (1 Cor. 10:16–17). That's why it doesn't make sense to take communion on our own. The very word *communion* informs what's taking place. We're communing with God *and* with each other. We're remembering that we've been reconciled not only to God but also to those around us.

A Greater Display of God's Glory

God's inherent glory never increases or diminishes. But that glory is more visible when we meet together to worship him. When we come together to "pour forth the fame of [God's] abundant goodness" (Ps. 145:7) through singing, praying, serving, and preaching, more people can see that God is worthy of praise.

As theologian Donald Whitney explains:

> When a football team wins the national championship, it gets more glory if the game is shown to millions throughout the country than if no one but you were to see it individually on closed-circuit TV. . . . Public glory obviously brings more glory than does private glory. Likewise, God gets more glory when you worship him with the church than when you worship him alone.[6]

It's through the church that the manifold wisdom of God is put on display (Eph. 3:10). God is glorified through his people, not simply individuals. David communed with God alone while guarding his flocks, but even he says,

> I will thank you in the great congregation;
>   in the mighty throng I will praise you. (Ps. 35:18)

He doesn't want to keep God's glory to himself as he composes a psalm in the middle of a field. He wants to share it with others.

It's important to remember that God receives more glory from our gatherings only as they're intentionally God-glorifying. If we don't clearly proclaim and treasure the gospel in those times, they won't glorify God. If Scripture doesn't govern, fuel, and fill our times together, they don't bring glory to God. If those who participate in our meetings gossip about each other, look down on each other, and would rather not be together, then our gatherings won't bring more glory to God. In fact, Paul rebuked the Corinthians for that very reason and told them their meetings were doing more harm than good (1 Cor. 11:17).

But if we meet as God intended—to sing, pray, read, hear, and obey his Word, to proclaim his praise in song, and to rehearse, revel in, and respond to the gospel—then we'll be glorifying God in a greater way than if we did those things alone.

EMBRACING THESE BENEFITS

These benefits of gathering with the church (and there are many others) call for a response. If I really think meeting with God's people is important and valuable, what difference will it make?

First, *I'll show up on time*. That might mean going to bed earlier on Saturday night to make sure my heart is at peace when I arrive Sunday morning. I'll want to arrive before the meeting starts and stay late, knowing that there are ample opportunities for God to work on either side of every meeting. By the way, if you're always five minutes late, it's not when you arrive that's the problem, but the time you leave your home.

Second, *I'll pray*. I'll pray that I hear and encounter God through his people. I'll pray that my heart is ready both to serve and to receive from others. One pastor I know prays through his membership directory regularly. Your church may be too large to do that, but that doesn't mean we can't pray consistently for *some* members, and especially our leaders.

Third, *I'll be prepared*. Some churches post the sermon text or songs for the coming Sunday in advance on their website. That gives members an opportunity to read and meditate on the passage beforehand and review the songs. But even if you don't know what's coming, you can prepare by singing or praying in the car on your way there, talking about what you're looking forward to, or thinking about the people who'll be there.

Fourth, *I'll seek to receive*. It should be clear by now that if we haven't come to receive, we won't have anything to give. This isn't self-centered Christianity. It's acknowledging that we have no resources in ourselves, and that from him, through him, and to him are all things (Rom. 11:35–36). God has strength, grace, faith, hope, and love he's eager to impart to us through the gospel every week in the power of his Spirit. So we come with open hands and hearts.

Fifth, *I'll seek to serve*. The gathered church was never meant to be a spectator event, with a few people in the spotlight and everyone else looking on. We're the body of Christ, being built up as each part is working properly (Eph. 4:16). More on this in the next chapter.

Sixth, *I'll seek to respond*. We're missing the point of gathering together if we see it as an end in itself. The songs we sing, the sermons we hear, the fellowship we share are all meant to prepare us for living each day for the glory of God as true worshipers. Right after Peter highlights our identity as the people of God (1 Pet. 2:9–10), he emphasizes the effect we're to have on our communities, workplaces, and neighborhoods:

Beloved, I urge you as sojourners and exiles to abstain from the passions of the flesh, which wage war against your soul. Keep your conduct among the Gentiles honorable, so that when they speak against you as evildoers, they may see your good deeds and glorify God on the day of visitation. (1 Pet. 2:11–12)

Meeting together is an event to look forward to as well as preparation for the rest of the week. In a continual cycle of the church gathering, then scattering, we find the relentless grace of God empowering us to live all of life for the glory of God.

DON'T NEGLECT MEETING

Every Sunday morning there are dozens of voices trying to convince us there's something better to give our time to than meeting with God's people. Sleeping in. Cramming for an exam. Playing golf. Catching up on housework. Enjoying a late brunch.

Don't believe them. There's no context or group on earth quite like the gathering of God's people. God has uniquely designed the church for true worshipers to experience, enjoy, and be edified by their common life in Christ. Every time we meet, God is eager and able to do more than we can ask or think according to the power at work within us (Eph. 3:20). There are no normal Sundays. Just fresh opportunities to behold the glory of the Lord as we're "transformed into the same image from one degree of glory to another" (2 Cor. 3:18).

God intends our gatherings to be a significant means of grace to strengthen us. But being on the receiving end of others' gifts is only one way we benefit from being together. In the next chapter we'll explore how God intends to bless us by using our gifts to strengthen others.

TRUE WORSHIPERS *EDIFY*

WORSHIP AND MATURITY

When you come together, each one has a hymn, a lesson, a revelation, a tongue, or an interpretation. Let all things be done for building up.

1 CORINTHIANS 14:26

Years ago I remember seeing a magazine ad for a Christian record label. The ad featured a thirty-something woman seated in a chair. With closed eyes and a contented smile, she seemed oblivious to anything around her as she listened to music under headphones. The caption simply stated, "WORSHIP."

Each time I saw it I had the same impression. The heart of worship involves blocking everyone and everything out and simply focusing on God while listening to music. I don't know if that's what the ad was supposed to communicate or not. I do know it's not what Scripture communicates.

In the last chapter, we saw how worshiping God as part of the redeemed community results in innumerable benefits. As we meet with each other, we meet with God. We aren't meant to block people out or avoid them. They're a primary way we receive from God.

In this chapter I want to focus in on the means of grace God wants us to be to others. It's true that worship is ultimately about God, but one of the most important ways we worship God is by building up other members of the body. Pastor and author Bryan Chapell sheds more light on this reality:

> Making God the exclusive goal of worship sounds very reverent but actually fails to respect Scripture's own gospel priorities. Certainly it is true that God is the most important audience member for our worship. But if God were not concerned for the good of his people, his glory would be diminished. He expects us not only to praise his name (Psalm 30:4), but also to teach, admonish, and encourage one another in worship (Colossians 3:16; Hebrews 10:24).[1]

God never intended that he be the only one concerned for the good of his people. He invites us to join him.

TWO SIDES OF THE SAME COIN

Apparently being concerned for others was a foreign idea to the church in first-century Corinth. They had written the apostle Paul asking him about "spiritual things." Some of the Corinthians were enamored with personal ecstatic experiences and took pride in healings, miracles, and speaking to God in unknown languages. They looked down on more mundane gifts, like helps or administration. They wanted

Paul to weigh in on this burning question: Who are the *really* spiritual people?

Paul's response in 1 Corinthians 12–14 shows us how badly the Corinthians had missed the mark. When you gather as the church to meet with God, Paul says, keep each other in view—that actually glorifies God. And it's why the word Paul uses to describe the purpose of our meetings isn't *worship*, but *edification*.

To edify means to build up. Edification can take place through a variety of means, but the result is always the same. People are strengthened, encouraged, and helped. Worship and edification are two sides of the same coin. When we serve others for their good, we're bringing glory to God. And when we exalt God through our expressions of praise, prayer, and thanks, we're building up those around us. At least, that's the way God intends it to work.

We typically think of edification as the responsibility of those who serve publicly, like the musicians and the pastor. They're supposed to edify us. This attitude is revealed in our comments: "The sermon seemed a little long today." "I thought the soloist did a great job this morning." "I wish they'd sing some songs I know." "I really liked the way the pastor prayed." "The band seemed a little off." We evaluate the quality of our time together based on the actions of others, not our own.

But God wants us to come to meetings asking how *we* can serve. "To *each* is given the manifestation of the Spirit for the common good" (1 Cor. 12:7). "Strive to excel in *building up* the church" (14:12). "Let all things be done for *building up*" (14:26).

It cuts across the grain of our consumeristic, self-centered culture to think that exalting God involves serving others. It certainly wasn't the mind-set of the Corinthians, who had become—among other things—highly individualistic in their thinking. In response, Paul spelled out four priorities that would help them pursue mutual edification as a way of exalting God. They're just as relevant today as they were in the first century.[2]

THE PRIORITY OF VARIETY

Paul begins by making it clear that God chooses to exalt himself in a variety of ways when we gather. There are different gifts, different kinds of service, and different activities, all given by the one triune God (1 Cor. 12:4–6).

Some of us are tempted to think our contribution isn't very important. We compare ourselves to more-gifted people and look like losers. Or at least nonessential participants. We don't think the church needs our gifts, so we drift, mentally, emotionally, or relationally. It's a perspective that easily morphs into self-pity.

Paul addresses those who think they're unneeded with these words: "If the foot should say, 'Because I am not a hand, I do not belong to the body,' that would not make it any less a part of the body" (12:15). Significant differences exist between feet and hands. Feet are walked on, get dirty, are hidden under shoes or socks, and smell bad. Hands do important stuff. We use our hands to build things, play an instrument, catch a ball, comfort a friend. What do you extend when you greet someone? Your hand. What do we use to create great works of art, write a love letter, or make a meal? Our hands.

Feet people can become discouraged hanging around hand people. But if your foot seems peripheral to your body, just wait until you sprain your ankle or break a toe. Suddenly, your foot is crucial. You realize that without feet it's difficult for your hands to go anywhere. Both our hands *and* our feet are important.

Paul shares another analogy to communicate the same point: "And if the ear should say, 'Because I am not an eye, I do not belong to the body,' that would not make it any less a part of the body" (12:16). But Paul says it would be a disaster if the whole body were an eye. We'd be rolling around on the floor, seeing a lot but unable to make any difference.

What gift do you view as the "eye" or "hand"? For some people it's being the pastor. For others it's being one of the musicians on Sunday morning. You might have thoughts of becoming a deacon or the head usher. I don't know.

What I do know is that God gifts different people in different ways, and every gift is important for his glory. God has designed you for specific purposes. You may not be able to serve in the way you *want* to serve, but there's no question that God has given you gifts to serve somewhere.

That's why Paul says in verse 18 that "God arranged the members in the body . . . as he chose." This is God's design, not ours. Our unity is strengthened and displayed as we appreciate the diverse ways God has made us.

There are no nongifted, dispensable people in the church. Every member of the body of Christ, and every member of a local church, is "unique, distinctive, irreplaceable, unrepeatable," as British pastor David Prior expresses it.[3] Just as there is no body part we'd be happy to lose, there is no one in the church who doesn't have a purpose in God's plan.

But what happens when those with certain gifts are puffed up? While some people struggle with self-pity and say, "I'm not really needed," others tend toward self-exaltation—and conclude that they're the only ones who are truly needed. Comparing themselves to others, they come out on top. So Paul gives this reminder: "The eye cannot say to the hand, 'I have no need of you,' nor again the head to the feet, 'I have no need of you'" (12:21).

"Eyes" and "head" seem to represent those in leadership or prominent roles—here literally looking down on the "hands" and "feet," those in serving roles. The temptation is for those in prominent positions to think their contribution is sufficient, unique, or better. They think other parts, or members, aren't needed like they are.

That attitude is repulsive to God. He intends that we both enjoy and benefit from the gifts of others—not despise them, ignore them, or wish they didn't exist. New Testament scholar David Garland, in his commentary on 1 Corinthians, writes: "The persons with deceptively ordinary and unprestigious gifts are as necessary for the proper functioning of the community as those who put on a more glittery display. All are of equal value."[4]

That's why churches aren't meant to be built upon or around two or three public gifts like teaching or leading music. God didn't design the church to be a group of spectators watching others perform. Everyone is needed. Everyone participates.

Imagine if each Sunday the only gifts exercised in your church were those up front. There would be no greeters, no children's workers, no administrators, no setup team, no sound personnel, no gifts of hospitality, generosity, or mercy. You might have a crowd. But you wouldn't have a church.

For years, my pastor and dear friend, C. J. Mahaney, has made it a practice to turn around and thank the musicians after he's given the benediction and the meeting is over. He recognizes his gift of teaching, while significant, isn't the only gift God has placed in the church. That's the fruit of recognizing God's priority of variety in the church. It leads to a culture of gratefulness and celebration, because we know that the diverse gifts we benefit from are gracious gifts from an intentional, loving, and wise God.

THE PRIORITY OF LOVE

Another priority when we think about edifying others is love. For Paul, the aspect of love in our meetings and lives is so important that he takes an entire thirteen verses in 1 Corinthians 13 to spell it out. In one of the most quoted passages of Scripture, Paul puts serving without love in the worst possible light.

Loveless speech is like beating on a trash-can lid. You can prophesy, understand mysteries, and have encyclopedic knowledge, but if it lacks love, it means nothing. You can exercise great faith toward God for people, resulting in significant changes and progress, but if love isn't behind it, it's useless. You can give sacrificially, even lay down your life to be martyred, but if it's not because you're expressing love, again, it has no value.

Those are sobering words. But how do we know when our efforts to build up others lack love? We lack love when we serve others to gain glory for ourselves rather than Jesus.

That's most often revealed to us when our contributions are either criticized or passed over.

I remember years ago, pre-Internet, putting dozens of hours into publishing a church newsletter. After about three months I turned the leadership over to someone else. When the pastor publicly commended the newsletter team one Sunday morning, he didn't mention me. I don't know if it was intentional or an oversight. It didn't matter. My cheeks flushed with anger. *How could he not notice my contribution? I've slaved away behind closed doors to get this thing off the ground. Not even a mention? I can't believe it!*

My serving might have started as an act of love. But my response that morning revealed that it had become an act of self-exaltation. And when I didn't get the glory I wanted, I fumed. Serving for the glory of Jesus overlooks those kinds of "offenses." We're just happy that someone's doing work that builds up God's people.

Whenever I'm tempted to discouragement, anger, bitterness, comparison, or envy by someone else's serving, it's a sure sign that *my* serving lacks love and brings no glory to God.

We also lack love when we're insensitive to how what we're doing or the way we're doing it might affect others. I've talked to more than one leader who confessed discouragement as they looked out on the bored facial expressions of their congregation. Have you ever considered that your face and body are a means of encouraging and building up not only your leaders but those around you?

Sometimes even well-intentioned actions can affect those around us negatively. If you're the only person in the room jumping up and down with your hands raised high, you might want to consider whether you're leading people to think more about Jesus or about you. My wife has mentioned to me on more than one occasion that I was singing so loudly, it was distracting. Singing isn't just about how I feel toward Jesus. It's about how I feel toward those around me as well. Being aware of others is just one more way of bringing glory to the Savior.

The priority of love is important when we interact with leaders as well. When we express concern or disagreement with something that took place, are we seeking to build up or simply correct? To strengthen or to criticize? To bless or stand in judgment?

The reason love is a priority in the way we serve others is that this is the way God has served us. He loved us so much that he sent his Son to rescue us from our sure damnation. "By this we know love, that he laid down his life for us, and we ought to lay down our lives for the brothers" (1 John 3:16).

The more we understand the depths of love God has shown us, the more we'll want to serve others with that same love.

THE PRIORITY OF INTELLIGIBILITY

Another priority in building others up is intelligibility. Can people understand what we're doing and saying as the church meets? Or do guests feel like they're entering a secret club where only longtime members get what's going on?

Paul gives us startlingly simple illustrations in 1 Corinthians 14:6–11 to make this point. If someone plays a musical instrument and no one can make out what the sounds are, how will anyone be able to say what piece is being played?

While some would call that modern music, Paul says it's unhelpful. If a bugle call summons an army to battle but the sound is indistinct, the army might be headed for a crushing defeat. If we use words that others can't understand, how is that helping them?

I've been in contexts where a church had grown so used to certain expressions, forms, or patterns that newcomers had little chance of understanding what was happening. Guests shouldn't feel that if they don't know the code words, they'll be lost. Words like *surety, missional, redeemed, legalistic, sharing,* and *interpose* might not be as understandable to the surrounding culture as they are to us. Even more common words like *glory, grace, blood,* and *gospel* can bear explanation, especially when used in conversations.

Aspects of a meeting such as where to take your children, what to say and when to say it, the order of the meeting, and what's expected of guests can all be stumbling blocks to a visitor. At the end of 1 Corinthians 14 Paul uses the example of the confusing sound of tongues to stress the importance of intelligibility. Even churches that don't believe in that particular gift might need the gift of interpretation to help those who are visiting.

As we seek to be clearly understood, God can use us to build up others for his glory.

THE PRIORITY OF THE GOSPEL

While the things we do as God's people bring him glory, they're meant to point to what God has done to *make* us his people. And what he has done is sent Jesus Christ to redeem us. That's why after an extended discourse on how we're to build each other up when we gather, Paul reminds the Corinthians of what is of first importance: the gospel. Jesus Christ has come, died, and risen from the dead, just as the Scriptures promised (1 Cor. 15:3–4).

God is interested in not only edifying us as individuals but also building us *together* into Christ. Our relationships, our connectedness, our bonds matter to God. He wants them strong. We're not bricks on a construction site piled up randomly. That's not a building. It's a stack of bricks. Someone could come by and easily knock them all down. They bring no safety, security, or protection to anyone.

God wants to strengthen the spiritual mortar that binds us together. That mortar is Jesus Christ himself. Those who worship God in spirit and truth continually return to the gospel of Jesus Christ. "Therefore, as you received Christ Jesus the Lord, so walk in him, rooted and built up in him and established in the faith, just as you were taught, abounding in thanksgiving" (Col. 2:6–7).

If we're built up by being rooted and grounded in Christ, the best way to edify others through our serving is to build them more into Christ. In other words, rather than drawing attention to ourselves, we seek to draw people's attention to who Jesus is and what he's accomplished. We don't serve one another so people will notice us. Rather, we use our gifts to the fullest to exalt the Giver of those gifts.

So everything we do is meant to help others see what Jesus Christ has done and why it matters. We serve out of gratefulness that Christ has served us (Luke 22:27). We comfort others with the comfort we've received from knowing our sins are forgiven (2 Thess. 2:16–17). We encourage others to trust God, knowing that he who gave up his Son for us will graciously give us all things (Rom. 8:32). We pray confidently to God, aware that Jesus himself intercedes for us (8:34). We outdo one another in showing honor because we've received the unimaginable honor of being called children of God (Rom. 12:10; 1 John 3:1). We welcome one another as Christ has welcomed us, for the glory of God (Rom. 15:7). In every way possible we draw attention to the grace we've been shown in the gospel, bringing glory to God in the process.

True worshipers have the good of others in view because they have Christ's glory in view. The two are inseparable. We should never think about exalting God without thinking about serving and building up others as well.

Of all the ways God has given us to build up those around us when we meet, few have caused more turmoil and tension throughout the centuries than singing together. We turn to that topic next.

6

TRUE WORSHIPERS *SING*

WORSHIP AND MUSIC

> Let the word of Christ dwell in you richly, teaching and
> admonishing one another in all wisdom, singing psalms
> and hymns and spiritual songs, with thankfulness in your
> hearts to God.
>
> COLOSSIANS 3:16

Years ago one of my neighbors visited our church. When I
asked his wife how they liked it, she responded, "It was good,
but my husband won't be coming back."

"Why?" I asked.

"You sing too much, and he doesn't like to sing."

I regretted her decision but appreciated her evaluation.
We did sing a lot.

I've been singing for as long as I can remember. I partici-
pated in choirs in high school and college, and traveled with
the Christian group GLAD for twelve years. I've been leading
worship in song for more than thirty-five years. I love to sing.

But I realize that not everyone shares my background. You may have seen the title of this chapter and winced. *Me, sing? You've got to be kidding.* Maybe you're like my neighbor years ago. Singing just doesn't "do it" for you.

Then there are Christians who never stop singing. They can drive you nuts. They sing when they wake up, in the shower, as they're making breakfast, driving to school or work, and throughout the day. They sing along with TV show themes, commercials, the radio, their iPod (usually too loud), and at concerts. Oh, and at church, too.

I also have friends who are ambivalent toward singing. It's fine that people do it, but for them singing falls in the category of nice but not necessary.

So when it comes to Christians and singing, we have the trained and passionate, as well as the nongifted, the unaffected, and the disinterested. And I'm sure there are more categories. Does God want every Christian to sing?

It depends. If singing were an issue of training, technique, vocal range, comfort, or preference, most of us would be wise to keep our mouths shut. The world would be a more pleasant and happier place. Why sing when so many are more gifted and seem to enjoy it more than we do?

Here's why. Your voice, along with all the other voices in your church, has been redeemed by the Savior. As we sing, he presents our song to the Father for his glory and our joy. "The human voice, given over to Jesus, and found in company with other voices given over similarly, produces a dignified and worthy song from storefront church to cathedral," says Harold Best. "Singing is not an option for the Christian; no one is excused. Vocal skill is not a criterion."[1]

No one is excused. Not even those with zero musical ability. The critical question is not Do I have a voice? but Do I have a song? And if you're a true worshiper, forgiven and reconciled to God through the atoning work of Christ, the answer is a resounding *yes*. It's not a song we originated or created. We can't add to it, change it, or improve upon it. It's the song of the redeemed for their great Redeemer.

It's a song we were never meant to sing alone. And as we'll see, it's a song God's people have been singing together for thousands of years.

THE SONG OF REDEMPTION

We hear the first strains of salvation's song when God delivers his people through the Red Sea in Exodus 15. As the once-fearsome Egyptian army drowns and their bodies wash up on the seashore (Ex. 14:30), the whole nation of Israel breaks out into exuberant musical worship:

> I will sing to the LORD, for he has triumphed gloriously;
> > the horse and his rider he has thrown into the sea.
> The LORD is my strength and my song,
> > and he has become my salvation;
> this is my God, and I will praise him,
> > my father's God, and I will exalt him. (Ex. 15:1–2)

Years later, the song of redemption continues to resonate in the Psalms as God's people praise the One who

> saved them from the hand of the foe
> > and redeemed them from the power of the enemy.
> > > (Ps. 106:10)

And the singing isn't occasional. David assigns Levite musicians to sing God's praises day and night at the temple (1 Chron. 9:33; 15:19–22). That's because God wants us to do more than praise him for saving us. He wants us to *sing* those praises.

> Oh sing to the LORD a new song;
>> sing to the LORD, all the earth!
> Sing to the LORD, bless his name;
>> tell of his salvation from day to day. (Ps. 96:1–2)

The majestic melody continues as the exiles returning from Babylon are commanded,

> Break forth together into singing,
>> you waste places of Jerusalem,
> for the LORD has comforted his people;
>> he has redeemed Jerusalem. (Isa. 52:9)

There are always fresh reasons to "sing to the LORD a new song" (Ps. 96:1; Isa. 42:10).

In the New Testament, the apostle Paul tells us that songs enable the word of Christ, the great Redeemer, to dwell in our hearts richly (Col. 3:16). That explains why Paul and Silas, after being stripped and beaten and tossed in a Philippian prison, were singing hymns to God (Acts 16:25). Even in the midst of persecution they had a song to sing that circumstances couldn't silence.

The song of redemption continues into the new heavens and new earth. There every heart, hand, and voice will be raised in passionate praise to the Lamb who was slain, who by his blood

ransomed people for God
> from every tribe and language and people and nation.
>> (Rev. 5:9)

If you no longer have to fear eternal separation from God, if death is merely the doorway to unspeakable joy, if sin has been conquered, hell is overcome, and Jesus has saved you to enjoy unending pleasures at God's right hand, then you have a song to sing. And it's a song that no trial, no disease, no struggle, no persecution, no power on earth or in hell can stop.

SO WHY DO WE *SING*?

This brief scriptural survey still leaves us asking, Why do we *sing*? Why not recite sonnets? Or wave banners with Scripture verses written on them? Or dance? Or knock pieces of wood together? Why repeatedly subject Christians to the often awkward, out-of-tune, halting sounds of congregational singing? Why don't we follow the counsel of C. S. Lewis who suggested, "What I, like many other laymen, chiefly desire in church are fewer, better, and shorter hymns; especially fewer."[2]

It's an important question. If we sing without understanding God's purpose for it, we won't be motivated to sing. We won't benefit in the ways God intends us to. Most of all, God won't be glorified by our singing.

One reason we sing is that God tells us to. A quick word study shows that there are more than four hundred verses in Scripture that reference singing, including almost fifty direct exhortations to sing. Four of them are concisely contained in Psalm 47:6:

> Sing praise to God, sing praises!
> Sing praises to our King, sing praises!

One could start to wonder if the Bible was written specifically for musicians. It wasn't.

Another reason singing plays a prominent role in Scripture is that all three persons of the Trinity are connected with song. Zephaniah 3:17 says that the Father will exult over his people "with loud singing." Jesus sings with his disciples after the Last Supper, and most likely sang every week as he attended synagogue (Matt. 26:30; Luke 4:16). In Hebrews, these words from Psalm 22 are placed in Jesus's mouth: "In the midst of the congregation I will sing your praise" (Heb. 2:12). Singing psalms, hymns, and spiritual songs is tied to being filled with the Holy Spirit in such an integral way that it can be hard to determine which is the cause and which is the effect (Eph. 5:19). God wants us to sing because *he* sings.

WHAT SINGING DOES

Knowing that Scripture encourages our singing and that God sings is one thing. Knowing *how* we're to sing is another. Because we can sing badly. We can sing for the wrong reasons. We can lack motivation. We can sing without knowing what we're supposed to do besides make sounds with our mouths.

Two passages in the New Testament specifically address singing:

> And do not get drunk with wine, for that is debauchery, but be filled with the Spirit, addressing one another in psalms and hymns and spiritual songs, singing and making melody to the Lord with your heart, giving thanks always and for

everything to God the Father in the name of our Lord Jesus Christ. (Eph. 5:18–20)

And let the peace of Christ rule in your hearts, to which indeed you were called in one body. And be thankful. Let the word of Christ dwell in you richly, teaching and admonishing one another in all wisdom, singing psalms and hymns and spiritual songs, with thankfulness in your hearts to God. And whatever you do, in word or deed, do everything in the name of the Lord Jesus, giving thanks to God the Father through him. (Col. 3:15–17)

These provide a starting point for understanding more clearly why God wants us to sing.

Singing encourages and expresses the Spirit's work in our hearts. When Paul wants to describe our singing, he reaches for an unexpected analogy: getting drunk. That's because our singing has a source. In Ephesians 5:18 he compares being filled with spirits to being filled with the Spirit. They both refer to something that affects your behavior. That's where the phrase "driving under the influence" comes from. Being filled with alcohol and being filled with the Holy Spirit can both lead to unhindered expressions of joy and enthusiasm.

But that's where the similarities end. Paul isn't commending being "drunk with the Spirit," falling on the floor, using slurred speech, and having to be carried to our cars. That's not what this passage is saying or supporting. Paul is stressing differences more than similarities. Alcohol is a depressant. It dulls the brain and the senses. Too much liquor in the bloodstream results in loss of control, discernment, and balance. It can lead to debased sensuality. In contrast, the Holy Spirit, in the words of D. Martyn Lloyd-Jones, is a stimulant. He gives new life. He makes Christ glorious in our eyes. He reveals the love of God to us. He brings self-control, wisdom, understanding, and discernment. He makes us behave at our very best and brightest. And he makes us want to sing.

We want to be continually under the influence of the Spirit. And surprisingly, one of the ways God intends for us to experience the Spirit's influence is through singing. Singing that builds up the church, affects our hearts, exalts Christ, and makes us aware of God's presence.

If the Spirit of God is so connected to our songs of praise, that has implications. We don't have to wait for the worship leader or band to persuade us to sing. We don't have to warm up or be convinced that lifting our voices is good for us. The Spirit already indwells us as believers and is eager to fill our mouths with psalms, hymns, and spiritual songs. And we can expect that as we sing, in a small group or large, God's Spirit will be at work in supernatural ways, transforming us into the image of Christ from one degree of glory to the next (2 Cor. 3:18).

Singing helps us remember God's Word. Colossians 3:16 says that we're to let the word of Christ dwell richly in us as we sing psalms, hymns, and spiritual songs. This "word of Christ" is Paul's way of referring to the gospel. It's the good news about Jesus, the risen Savior who has come in the flesh to endure God's wrath in our place and reconcile us to God. That news with all its implications is meant to dwell richly in our hearts and minds as we sing. "Christ is the ground and the content of Christian song. Christians sing about Christ. If they sing about God, it is especially what God has done through Christ; if about the Holy Spirit, it is the Holy Spirit as the gift of Christ; if about instruction to one another, it is the life in Christ."[3]

The Colossians would have understood Paul to be saying that God wants the gospel to dwell in us so deeply that we're influenced, shaped, and governed by it. So why the mention of music?

Music helps us remember words—and God intends for music to help us remember the word of Christ.

Dr. Oliver Sacks has studied the effect of music on the brain for years. In his book *Musicophilia* he writes, "Every culture has songs and rhymes to help children learn the alphabet, numbers, and other lists. Even as adults, we're limited in our ability to memorize series or to hold them in mind unless we use mnemonic devices or patterns—and the most powerful of these devices are rhyme, meter, and song."[4]

An Alzheimer's patient fails to recognize his wife or children but joins in enthusiastically when he hears a song he learned as a teenager. Jingles get stuck in our head for hours, if not days. A song we hadn't heard for decades starts playing in a store and we instinctively start mouthing the lyrics.

God himself used music as a means to help people remember his Word. As the Israelites were about to enter the Promised Land, God told Moses to teach them a song so that "when many evils and troubles have come upon them, this song shall confront them as a witness (for it will live unforgotten in the mouths of their offspring)" (Deut. 31:21). We remember what we sing.

Since music already serves us as a memory tool, most of us can probably make better use of it. Saints throughout history have learned dozens if not hundreds of hymns by heart. Few people I know can say the same. I've watched people keep their eyes glued to the screen or printed page even when they're singing songs they've already memorized. We know the words but continue to stare at them anyway. If that's your habit, try reading a line of a song and then looking away as you sing the line from your heart. You can also try taking time during your devotions to review songs. You'll be surprised how quickly you'll be committing them to memory.

Singing helps us remember God's Word. Let's take advantage of all it can do.

Singing helps us teach and be taught. The primary way we're taught when we gather is through a pastor faithfully expositing God's Word. But Paul tells us in Colossians 3 that as we sing, we also "teach and admonish one another." While singing involves me, it's never just about me. While we make melody to the Lord in our hearts, we also address one another in song (Eph. 5:19). There's a vertical as well as a horizontal focus to our singing. Instruction is taking place right alongside praise.

God allows for variety in the way mutual instruction can take place. Half of the congregation can sing to the other half. A leader can lead a call and response. A soloist or group of vocalists can sing while the rest of the church is fed and inspired. Most often though, singing to one another means singing together, every heart "making melody to the Lord."

Here's how the teaching takes place. When we sing, "Though the eye of sinful man thy glory may not see," we're counseling each other that our sins have caused a separation between us and God that we can't close ourselves. The words "You give and take away" teach us that whether God brings us to a place of abundance or lack, we can still bless the Lord. With the lyrics "Because the sinless Savior died, my sinful soul is counted free" we're admonishing each other not to live in condemnation for sins that the Savior has already paid for. "Riches I heed not, nor man's empty praise" instructs us in the futility of living for fleeting wealth or the applause of others. Singing is meant to be an educational event.[5]

It's not uncommon to walk into a worship meeting distracted and weighed down by anxiety, relational struggles, discouragement, or condemnation. As we sing with the church, we often let biblical truths enter our ears and pass through our lips with no effect. In so doing, we don't allow Christ-centered, biblically faithful songs to encourage and equip us in our common battles and temptations.

It may be because we're expecting the music alone to affect our souls and perspective. While music speaks to our emotions, it's the truth that sets us free, not music. New Testament scholar Douglas Moo writes, "Worship of God should always involve the emotions; how can we praise a holy God who has redeemed us without getting emotional about it? But what should move our emotions is not the sonorous tones of the organ or the insistent beat of the drums, but the mind's apprehension of truth about God."[6]

If our songs are meant to teach us, then focusing on the words we sing matters. Biblical realities are more significant than the melodies we use to sing them. Or put more simply, truth transcends tunes.

One way to grow in our appreciation for the lyrics of the songs is to take time to read and meditate on them. We did this at various times with our children while they were growing up, and found that this greatly increased their engagement in the Sunday meeting. They actually had some idea of what we were singing about. And by the way, this works for adults, too.

Singing helps express and engage our emotions. The fact that singing has so much to do with words doesn't mean that emotions are unimportant. In every culture, in every age, music is a language of the heart. It expresses, arouses, and connects with what we feel. Paul makes that association when he says we're to make "melody to the Lord with [our] hearts," and sing "with thankfulness in [our] hearts to God" (Eph. 5:19; Col. 3:16).

Of course, words are sufficient in themselves for expressing emotions. But that again raises the question of why we sing at all. John Piper helps us understand:

> The reason we sing is because there are depths and heights and intensities and kinds of emotions that will not be satisfactorily expressed by mere prosaic forms, or even poetic readings. There are realities that demand to break out of prose into poetry and some demand that poetry be stretched into song. . . . Singing is the Christian's way of saying: God is so great that thinking will not suffice, there must be deep feeling; and talking will not suffice, there must be singing.[7]

"Talking will not suffice, there must be singing." How does music help us move beyond just talking?

First, singing enables us to reflect on the meaning of words. It can stretch out words, repeat them, or put space between them. These qualities can help us think more deeply about what we're singing. It's the difference between saying, "It is well with my soul," and singing the chorus of that song slowly, repeating the phrases multiple times.

Music can also amplify the emotions that lyrics are meant to convey. Whether it's joyful celebration, reverent awe, or sober repentance, music can be an additional influence that guides and deepens those emotions. Both "Happy Day" (Tim Hughes and Ben Cantelon) and "O Sacred Head Now Wounded" mention the cross but in two very different settings. The first song enables us to jubilantly celebrate Christ's death and resurrection with abandon, while the hymn reflects the profound grief we experience as we meditate on the need for Jesus to die for our sins. There's a reason each song was set to its particular tune.

Some Christians have been taught to repress their emotions as they sing. They've been told to fear feeling anything too strongly, and that maturity means holding back. But what we want to avoid is *emotionalism*, not *emotions*. Emotionalism pursues feelings as an end in themselves. It's wanting to feel something with no regard for how that feeling is produced or its ultimate purpose.

In contrast, the emotions that singing is meant to express are a response to who God is and what he's done. Vibrant singing enables us to combine truth *about* God seamlessly with passion *for* God. Doctrine and devotion. Mind and heart. Suppressing or ignoring your feelings when you sing contradicts what singing is designed to do. Passionless singing is an oxymoron.

"Let us remember," hymn writer Isaac Watts (1674–1748) tells us, "that the very power of singing was given to human nature chiefly for this purpose, that our own warmest affections of soul might break out into natural or divine melody, and that the tongue of the worshipper might express his own heart."[8]

The heart feelings music expresses aren't always happy ones. There are times when it's appropriate for the church to sing songs of lament that acknowledge the trials, temptations, and unanswered prayers of life. But the emotion most often connected in Scripture with singing is joy.

> Make a joyful noise to the LORD, all the earth;
>> break forth into joyous song and sing praises![9]

Woven through the struggles, uncertainties, doubts, fears, and failings of life is the redemptive melody of the glorious gospel. We're assured that God has chosen us as his own, that he's using every trial to conform us to the image of his Son, and that he'll keep us safe until we see him face to face.

And so we sing psalms, hymns, and spiritual songs with thankfulness in our hearts to God (Col. 3:16).

Singing encourages physical expressiveness. Singing is an act that requires more physical engagement than just listening, or even speaking. Our diaphragms, lungs, throats, and lips work together to produce musical sounds for the glory of God. That may be one reason the Psalms include other forms of bodily activity in our worship of God. We're invited to kneel, lift our hands, bow, clap, shout, play instruments, dance, and stand in awe as we seek to honor God (Pss. 33:1, 8; 47:1; 95:6; 134:2; 149:3; 150:3–5).

John Stott writes, "There is a place in public worship both for shouting aloud because he is the great God, and for bowing down before him because he is our God."[10] Both shouting and bowing are physical activities. The reality of God's presence calls for a response that's expressed through the totality of our being, so that we worship God with mind, soul, and body—with all that we are.

The fact that singing is often connected to physical expressiveness doesn't mean that everyone thinks the two should go together or that the expressiveness always looks the same. Cultures vary on what they consider appropriate physical expression. Brits and Aussies tend to be more reserved than Americans and Africans, for example. But in every culture you'll find believers who naturally respond to God's greatness and goodness with their bodies as well as their voices.

So let me suggest a few reasons why actively participating with our bodies while we sing is appropriate and biblical.

We follow scriptural examples and exhortations. While most examples of physical expression are found in the Psalms, the New Testament includes references to falling down, kneeling, and lifting hands as well (Acts 20:36; 1 Cor. 14:25; 1 Tim. 2:8). The abundance of passages implies that God views our bodies as one means to bring him glory as we sing.

We encourage others. Your voice isn't the only way you can teach and admonish others when you sing. Your emotional and bodily engagement can encourage others to think about the greatness of the God you're singing to. Psalm 34:5 says that those who look to the Lord "are radiant, / and their faces shall never be ashamed." When you sing to the Lord, would someone describe your countenance as radiant? Or something else?

We give fuller expression of our love for God. Why should expressions to God be limited to mere thoughts and words? That's unlike any other relationship. I don't sit across from Julie on our date night fearing someone might think I love her too much. I want others to know how I feel about her, and I don't limit that to words. I gaze at her, touch her, smile at her, hug her, interact with her. And actually, that's because I'm crazy about her, and not because we're in a public setting. I magnify her worth through my physical expressiveness. So we magnify the worth of God through our bodies. We say to those around us, "My God is so great, I will praise him with my whole being" (see Ps. 108:1–2).

We stir our own hearts. It can seem hypocritical to be physically expressive when you don't feel anything inside. But none other than John Calvin pointed out how helpful bodily posture and actions can be in encouraging our own souls:

> The inward attitude certainly holds first place in prayer, but outward signs, kneeling, uncovering the head, lifting up the hands, have a twofold use. The first is that we may employ all our members for the glory and worship of God; secondly, that we are, so to speak, jolted out of our laziness by this help. There is also a third use in solemn and public prayer, because in this way the sons of God profess their piety, and they inflame each other with reverence of God. But just as the lifting up of the hands is a symbol of confidence and longing, so in order to show our humility, we fall down on our knees.[11]

When we experience a lack of desire for God or an inner dullness, our greatest need is to fill our minds with truths about God, especially as he's revealed himself to us in the gospel. But our bodies are another way God has given us to stir up our hearts to respond rightly to his glory. Bowing my head, lifting my hands, or kneeling down can remind me of the humility, gratefulness, and awe I should feel that Jesus has redeemed me.

Singing helps us express our unity with the church. Paul uses the musical term *harmony* three times in his letters (Rom. 12:16; 15:5; Col. 3:14). In each case he's not referencing music. He's describing relational unity.

While gathering together is in itself an expression of our unity in Christ, singing together is an opportunity to deepen that expression and experience. Better than simply reciting or shouting words in unison, singing enables us to spend extended periods of time communicating the same thoughts, passions, and intentions to each other.

If singing together is meant to express our unity in Christ, that means every voice matters. Including yours. Personal headphones might now be a universal accessory, but they're out of place on Sunday mornings. In the church God calls us not simply to listen to others sing, but to sing ourselves. No one else might notice, but God hears every voice and heart distinctly (Heb. 4:12).

Knowing that singing is meant to express our unity in the gospel doesn't mean we'll always like the songs we sing. Paul's reference to "psalms, hymns, and spiritual songs" most likely indicates that the songs of the church will be varied.

One style of music will never fully capture the glories of God or our appropriate responses to him. Although conflicts over music styles in the church didn't exist in Paul's time, he wisely encouraged the Colossians in the context of singing to "let the peace of Christ rule in your hearts, to which indeed you were called in one body" (Col. 3:15). We sing as one body for God's glory.

That means there might be times when our most sincere worship is singing a song we don't prefer because we know someone else is helped by it. It's one way we can let the peace of Christ rule in our hearts and count others more significant than ourselves (Phil. 2:3)

In Revelation, the hosts of heaven are in unity not because of the style of music they're using but because of the focus of their song. Listen to it:

> Worthy is the Lamb who was slain,
> to receive power and wealth and wisdom and might
> and honor and glory and blessing! (Rev. 5:12)

What kind of music do God's children from every tribe and language and people and nation sing? We don't know. God hasn't told us. But we do know the focus: "Worthy is the Lamb who was slain!" That's a theme we can enthusiastically join in on, now—and forever.

TRUE WORSHIPERS *KEEP SINGING*

WORSHIP AND PERSEVERANCE

But I will hope continually
and will praise you yet more and more.
PSALM 71:14

We ended the last chapter with our eyes on eternity, where our hearts and voices will be joined in perfect and undistracted praise to the triune God. But it's painfully obvious—we're not there yet.

Years ago, I spoke at a conference that featured musical leaders from different churches. One evening I stood in the front row as we sang numerous songs filled with shallow theology, too much repetition, and a focus on our feelings and achievements for God. At least that's what it seemed like to me. To top it off, the presentation felt more slick than sincere.

I struggled for a few minutes, then realized I had a choice. I could continue to catalog all the things I thought were deficient in the song choices and leadership and simply hide my discontent. Or I could seek to exalt God.

By God's grace, and only after years of choosing the first option in similar settings, I went with the second. Kneeling down on the floor, I told God I was proud and asked him to help me see his glory more clearly. I started declaring who he was and why he was so great. I thanked him that Jesus was a mighty Savior who had come to purchase my forgiveness and adoption. After a few minutes my soul was renewed, my mind was fixed on God's mercy to me, and the leader was no longer my focus. Jesus was.

I tell that story to acknowledge that congregational singing isn't always easy. If it were, I wouldn't need to spend two chapters on it. We'd just do it. But the reality is, many Christians have a less-than-stellar experience every Sunday. The reasons are many. It could be poor leadership, weak doctrine, inexperienced musicians, emotionalism, and more.

But in every circumstance, a true worshiper worships God. That's the priority. So I thought it might be helpful to address some questions I've been asked through the years, questions that will aid us in maintaining the priority of exalting God in the midst of various distractions and challenges.

WHAT IF I CAN'T SING?

Not being able to sing can be defined in a number of ways. Some people have a condition that physically keeps them from making musical sounds, whether that's laryngitis or something more serious. Others have no musical training and have a hard time keeping up with anything but simple melodies and rhythms. Sometimes songs are pitched too high or too low. Maybe we're unfamiliar with the song being led. And some people are just tone deaf. For all those reasons and more, people can't sing.

It's significant that God tells us to sing and make "melody to the Lord with your heart" (Eph. 5:19). People hear what we sing with our voices, but God hears what we sing with our hearts. That means the first thing to do is make sure your heart is focused on the mercy God has shown us in Christ. That's what produces a song in the first place. Then focus on the truth of the words you're singing and what they mean for your life. If you can't physically make a sound, be encouraged by listening to those around you sing.

WHAT IF I DON'T FEEL LIKE SINGING?

Sometimes we come in on a Sunday morning and the last thing we want to do is sing. Maybe you spent the night caring for your sick three-year-old, or just found out you have a mysterious growth on your thyroid, or are struggling in your marriage. Perhaps you've been dealing with intense pain for years. Sometimes the only emotions you want to express are ones like anger, fear, disconnectedness, or despair. What then?

God gave us singing as a means not only of expressing our emotions but also of speaking to them. As David skillfully played his lyre, Saul's troubled spirit was calmed (1 Sam. 16:23). Job describes the music of the pipe as bringing joy; later he speaks of it as reflecting mourning (Job 21:12; 30:31). After acknowledging that he feels distant from God, David writes,

I will sing to the LORD
because he has dealt bountifully with me. (Ps. 13:6)

In Matthew 11:17, Jesus refers to music that made people want to dance or mourn. When we also actually sing, we increase the potential effect lyrics can have on our souls.

Jonathan Edwards, in his classic *A Treatise concerning Religious Affections*, speaks to this: "The duty of singing praises to God seems to be given wholly to excite and express religious affections. There is no other reason why we should express ourselves to God in verse rather than in prose and with music, except that these things have a tendency to move our affections."[1]

The "affections" he's referring to are more than momentary musical highs, produced by hearing a beat we like or a harmonic progression we find interesting. They're religious affections, which means we're engaged with God and his truth in a way that influences and affects our words, thoughts, and choices. When we sing biblically sound, gospel-informed lyrics, our affections for God can be deepened.

We won't always be moved in the same way or to the same degree when we sing. There may be times when we feel numb. But the answer isn't to stop singing. Crying out to God for grace to feel strong affections toward him is itself a sign of a true worship. And certainly more fruitful than gritting our teeth and accepting that condition as normal.

Singing can be the very means God uses to touch our hearts and move us toward faith again. The psalmist sings songs in the night even as he cries out,

> Why are you cast down, O my soul,
>   and why are you in turmoil within me? (Ps. 42:5, 11)

By God's grace and in God's timing, songs of lament and confession and longing will eventually give way to songs of gratefulness, hope, and faith as our vision of God and his love for us in Christ becomes clearer.

Sometimes concern for what other people think about our voices affects our desire to sing. You don't want to be a distraction, but it brings more glory to God when you sing enthusiastically because of his greatness than when you hold back because you fear what the person next to you thinks. If you're tone deaf, it might be good to restain yourself just a little. But not completely.

WHY DO WE SING SO MANY OLD SONGS (OR NEW SONGS)?

Objecting to songs simply because they're old is rooted in the same problem as objecting to new ones. We want to sing the songs we like. But the issue isn't how familiar we are with the songs. The issue is whether we're going to take every opportunity as true worshipers to exalt God.

Old songs can seem boring. They don't have to be. If we focus on the eternal realities behind the words we're singing, rather than on the music alone, our perspective changes. We start to see that while music may get tired, Jesus doesn't. Faith enables us to hear songs as if for the first time because they're only a faint reflection of the unending praises being sung around the throne. Familiar songs can help us press deeper into the unseen glories behind them that are imperishable, undefiled, and unfading (1 Pet. 1:4). We come to know the God whose mercies are new every morning, every hour, every moment.

On the other hand, new songs can seem intimidating. They don't have to be. Rather than thinking I have to sing every note of a song I don't know, I'll sometimes just listen to those who do know it. I'll let others teach and admonish me with their words. I've had some profound encounters with God in those instances. As I become familiar with the song, I'll start singing along. An unfamiliar song never needs to keep me from lifting my heart to exalt God.

WHAT IF I FEEL LIKE A HYPOCRITE WHEN I SING?

If you've ever felt like a hypocrite when singing with other believers, you're not alone. Who hasn't felt out of place at times, in the midst of a singing congregation? Everyone else looks so together, so happy, so sincere, so godly. In contrast, you're remembering the number of times this week you failed to keep a lid on your anger, clicked through to pornographic images, or studied Facebook instead of your Bible.

I recall one Sunday morning driving in with Devon, my then-teenage son, getting into one of our frequent conflicts. After arriving, I battled thoughts that I was a sorry excuse for a Christian. But as we sang, God graciously reminded me that I was basing his acceptance of me on my performance. I rightly felt bad about my sin against my son, but I wasn't moving on from there to receive God's forgiveness through Christ's finished work on the cross.

When we're convicted of our sin and respond by confessing it to God and resting in what Christ has done, we have every reason to sing! That's not being a hypocrite—that's living in the good of the gospel. True hypocrites don't struggle with their sin. They indulge in sin while publicly seeking to portray themselves as righteous. They intend to deceive.

We can also be tempted to feel like hypocrites when we sing songs with lyrics that express commitment or devotion beyond what we think is believable or appropriate. "In all I do I honor you," "I worship you with all my heart," "I have no longings for another," and similar phrases can sound empty to us when we know they're not absolutely true of us.

The Psalms contain numerous expressions of commitment that seem hyperbolic, if not downright hypocritical. For instance, Asaph says,

> Whom have I in heaven but you?
>> And there is nothing on earth that I desire besides you.
>> (Ps. 73:25)

David declares boldly,

> I will bless the LORD at all times;
>> his praise shall continually be in my mouth. (Ps. 34:1)

Really? Except when he sees Bathsheba. (More professions of faithfulness and desire are found in Pss. 16:2; 52:9; 75:9; 119:33.)

Wholehearted expressions can actually help align our hearts with what God has done in us through the gospel. We've been made new creations, and have turned from idols to serve the living and true God (1 Thess. 1:9). We're reminded of our need for God's grace and his faithful promises.

In *A Guide to Prayer*, Isaac Watts says,

> We can never be too frequent or too solemn in the general surrender of our souls to God and binding our souls by a vow to be the Lord's forever: to love him above all things, to fear him, to hope in him, to walk in his ways

in a course of holy obedience, and to wait for his mercy unto eternal life.[2]

Amen!

Those are the benefits. Here are two concerns.

First, if we're singing words of commitment while engaging in unrepentant sin, hoping to impress others or "fool" God through our spirituality, we're deceived. Singing worship songs doesn't "balance out" disobedience. If that's our perspective, then we *are* hypocrites. But Jesus came for hypocrites too. They can come to the foot of the cross and find forgiveness for their hypocrisy and grace to change. They can experience the fruit of repentance that enables them to express their devotion with joy and faith.

Second, expressions of unwavering commitment should be mixed with regular requests for God's grace to fulfill them. Otherwise we can think that our struggle against sin is already over. It isn't, and won't be until we see Jesus face-to-face. But we can be sure that God has written his law upon our hearts (Jer. 31:33), and our love for him is something he himself has placed in us through the gospel. So with profound gratefulness and amazement, we can sing, "My soul finds rest in God alone."

WHAT DO I DO WHEN I'M DISTRACTED?

Probably one of the greatest challenges we face in the church is distractions. It's enough to be distracted internally by our own thoughts, relational challenges, struggles, pains, and anxieties. But distractions can also be external. There might be a loud, musically deficient vocalist right behind you. You might have a leader or someone in the band who's particularly expressive or grumpy looking. It could be a constant stream of images behind projected lyrics or the child-care numbers flashing. It might be the temperature in the room. If you're a musician, you could be bothered by a bad mix.

It's the rare meeting that doesn't have something we can complain about. But for true worshipers, the question is always, How can I respond in a way that exalts God's glory in Christ in my mind, affections, and will?

Generally, the first thing we can do is acknowledge that we're easily distracted. It's a sign of our fallenness. Rather than criticizing what's taking place, we can confess our quickness to judge and lack of love for God. We aren't throwing discernment out the window. But discernment doesn't trump the opportunity to press through challenges and savor the sweetness of Christ as we sing.

After confessing your own inadequacies, ask God to help you think about his grace that allowed you to sing his praise at all. Remember, worship is a gift we receive before it's a task we perform. Apart from the substitutionary death of Christ we would be under God's righteous judgment and condemnation. But we aren't. And that's reason to sing through any obstacle we face, for the glory of God.

If you're distracted by the people around you, it can be helpful to think that Christ perfects both your offering and theirs. Imagine what our voices sound like to the holy God! It's like a three-year-old girl bringing a stick-figure drawing to her dad. "See, Daddy? I made this for you!" The father receives it joyfully not because of the quality, but because of the heart behind it. In our case, the Father accepts what we bring not only on the basis of our sincere hearts, but because Jesus has made our worship acceptable through his once-for-all perfect offering (1 Pet. 2:4–5).

There might be times when a leader does something or is responsible for something that distracts a large number of people. After examining your heart, it might be helpful to approach the leader about what you experienced. Start with anything you can express gratefulness for (the leader's faithfulness, joy, etc.), and then ask questions about the particular concern. Only then should you humbly voice your thoughts. Be specific and not sinfully judgmental. "The moving lights were distracting" will be received better than "Why are you so intent on bringing worldly, ungodly technologies into the church and giving a foothold for the Devil?" Share it in a way that makes it clear you're seeking to serve the church and not simply criticize or whine. Leaders don't always know how what they're doing affects people.

If your leader responds to your concerns, great. If not, it may be that the leader doesn't share your perspective or that you're making too much of the issue. (Believe it or not, that has happened a few times in church history.) It might also be because leaders often receive conflicting input from people in the congregation. Ultimately, they're accountable to God for the choices they make.

If the distractions you're experiencing are ongoing and related to theological concerns, it would be good to have a serious conversation with not only the music leader, but your pastor also. Occasionally, you might have to wrestle with whether or not God is leading you to a different church. But take the time to pray and have humble conversations with your leaders before you make any decisions.

WHAT IF THE SONGS WE SING ARE THEOLOGICALLY SHALLOW?

While I pray that every church sings songs that are rich in the word of Christ, faithful to Scripture, and theologically engaging, I know that's not always happening. What do you do when your leaders pick songs that seem to be driven more by emotion and popularity than by their ability to feed our souls?

Shallow or vague lyrics need never prevent us from importing biblical truth into them. I've often sung additional words to myself when being led in songs. For example, if you're repeatedly singing a line like, "You are worthy of praise," tell the Lord the specific reasons why he's so worthy: "you redeemed me . . . you know all things . . . your mercies never end . . . you rule over all."

If you see this as an ongoing issue in your church, it would be most helpful to humbly approach your pastor to ask for his perspective. Who knows what God might do through your caring expressions of concern for the theological weight of the songs you sing?

WHAT DO I DO DURING INSTRUMENTAL BREAKS?

God has blessed the church with tens of thousands of songs that put words of praise, lament, celebration, awe, love, and joy on our lips. But what do we do when the instruments play for an extended portion of the song? Whether it's an instrumental solo, an extended turnaround, or a long ending, how can we respond?

What you don't want to do is become a spectator. Or an audience. Or a fan. Or just check out.

Our aim is to participate in the same way as when we sing: to exalt God in our hearts, minds, and bodies. There are different ways we can do that. To start, as we listen to the musicians play, we can thank God for the gift of skillfully played music. But we can do more. We can think about the words we've just been singing and take time to reflect on them. We can quote Scripture to ourselves. We can pray.

If you really want to be adventurous, and it won't seem too out of place in your church, you can take a phrase from the song you're singing and develop it. Express a line of the song as a prayer or respond to what you've just been singing. For example, during an instrumental break in "My Hope Is Built on Nothing Less," you might sing words like, "Thank you for being my rock, you never change, I can trust you in every trial, my hope is secure in you."

God never told us we can sing only when the words are projected or in the hymnal, and singing spontaneously can be a way to meditate on the truths we're proclaiming.

WHAT IF MY NEW CHURCH HAS A COMPLETELY DIFFERENT STYLE OR LITURGY?

Moving from one church to another can be a difficult process. We're introduced to new structures, new leaders, new ways of doing things, new songs, new surroundings, and new liturgics. Most of us are creatures of habit and prefer familiar surroundings to strange ones. But change provides an opportunity to discover where our foundations are and what we're truly trusting in. It also teaches us things about God we might not otherwise have known.

If you've moved from a large church to a small church, you'll find that God works in quiet, unspectacular ways as well as loud, impressive ways. If you've gone from a church with a formal liturgy to one that's less structured, you might be refreshed by more spontaneous expressions of praise. If you've gone the other direction, you might understand better how God makes his promised presence known through the normal means of preaching, prayer, Scripture reading, and the Lord's Supper.

True worshipers come to God through Christ in the power of his Spirit. And we do so in response to and under the authority of his Word. Everything else is means—various circumstances and methods by which we express our praise and devotion to God. In every situation God himself enables us to offer songs of confession, praise, gratefulness, and celebration through Jesus Christ.

May we see every hindrance, distraction, and trial as a fresh opportunity to declare the excellencies of him who called us out of darkness into his marvelous light.

8

TRUE WORSHIPERS *ENCOUNTER*

WORSHIP AND THE PRESENCE OF GOD

But if all prophesy, and an unbeliever or outsider enters, he is convicted by all, he is called to account by all, the secrets of his heart are disclosed, and so, falling on his face, he will worship God and declare that God is really among you.

1 CORINTHIANS 14:24–25

One of my favorite biographies is *Alexander Hamilton* by Ron Chernow. Hamilton (1757–1804) never served as an American president but had a greater impact than many who did. He was a fierce defender of the Constitution, and as the first secretary of the treasury, he laid the foundation for America's financial system.

While reading his story, I was enthralled. Hamilton had come alive to me. I felt as though I knew him and could predict what he would do in certain situations. From the very beginning I knew that Hamilton would eventually die in a duel of honor with Aaron Burr. But on page 708, when his life finally ended, I felt as if I'd lost a personal friend.

Since finishing the book, I've thought about Hamilton often. But obviously I've never expected to meet him. I never thought I'd hear his voice or bump into him at the grocery store. That's because Hamilton lived two centuries ago. He's dead. The only way I can encounter him now is on a lifeless page.

I wonder how many of us, when it comes to knowing and worshiping God, approach him like the main character of a biography. We learn what he did in the past but don't expect him to break into the present. We sing about God but don't expect to actually engage with him. We hear and read his Word, but it's no more than history, principles, commands, and promises in a book. A unique book, to be sure. But just a book.

The Bible isn't the biography of a distant, absent, or dead deity. Alexander Hamilton is dead; Jesus Christ is alive.

It can't be said often enough that the Bible is sufficient to provide all we need for a godly life. But God's presence and power aren't confined to it. Scripture speaks of a God who is near, a God who is active, a God who breaks into the present—a God with whom we can engage. A God who is personal. A God we can experience mentally, emotionally, and even physically at times.

By experiencing God physically, I'm not referring to shaking, strange coincidences, or emotional excesses. I'm talking about acknowledging and appreciating the fact that God is seeking true worshipers who not only believe things about him, but also know him as a God who is living, active, and with us. Not an idea, a philosophy, a social construct, a political system, or an inanimate object. True worshipers have a relationship with God that includes head knowledge but goes beyond it. Jesus is alive and wants us to know him. Personally.

Our worship isn't only *about* God; it *involves* God. It isn't only to and for God; it's the way we encounter and engage with God. The one who enables us to encounter God in the way I'm describing is God himself, in the person of the Holy Spirit.

THE HOLY SPIRIT AND GOD'S PRESENCE

Paul told the Philippians that believers are those who "worship by the Spirit of God and glory in Christ Jesus and put no confidence in the flesh" (Phil. 3:3). It's the Spirit who initially opens our eyes to see our sin and causes our hearts to trust in the Savior for complete forgiveness (John 3:5; 16:7–9; Rom. 8:15).

Just as we can't worship the Father apart from Jesus Christ, we can't worship him apart from the Holy Spirit. As one author starkly put it, "If worshipers are not consciously dependent upon the Holy Spirit, their worship is not truly Christian."[1]

The Holy Spirit's primary aim is to glorify Jesus by making us more like him (John 15:26; 16:14; 2 Cor. 3:18). He accomplishes that in a variety of ways. The Spirit confirms to us that we're children of God and shows us what God has freely given us (Rom. 8:15; 1 Cor. 2:12). He comforts us in our trials, enlightens us in our confusion, and empowers us for serving others, all for the Father's pleasure and the Son's glory (Acts 9:31; 1 Cor. 12:4; Heb. 6:4). In these ways and more the Spirit applies the gospel to our lives so that we might become more like the Savior who redeemed us and know the Father's love.

Another way the Spirit seeks to conform us to the image of Christ is by making us aware of his presence and power. J. I. Packer explains this:

The Spirit makes known the personal presence in and with the Christian and the church of the risen, reigning Savior. . . . He empowers, enables, purges, and leads generation after generation of sinners to face the reality of God. And he does it in order that Christ may be known, loved, trusted, honored and praised. . . .

The distinctive, constant, basic ministry of the Holy Spirit under the new covenant is . . . to mediate Christ's presence to believers.[2]

Theologian Wayne Grudem agrees when he says that a main role of the Holy Spirit "in the new covenant age is to manifest the presence of God, to give indications that make the presence of God known."[3]

How aware are you of the indications that God is present with us? How many times have you been with others in your church and wondered if God was even there? Should we expect any evidence that he's there? If so, what does that evidence look like? If true worshipers encounter God, is there anything we can do to help or hinder that encounter?

A DISTINGUISHING CHARACTERISTIC

For many Christians, encouragements to pursue God's presence leave them confused, anxious, or disinterested. Indeed, we can do everything we've talked about in this book—receive, exalt, gather, edify, sing—and still feel that God is distant or uninvolved.

We know we should be engaged with God, but we're not quite sure what that means. So we go through the motions. The Holy Spirit seems a bit like an appendix. He's there for something, but we're not quite sure what. And if we somehow lost him, things wouldn't be that different.

On the other hand, some believers make it sound like the Spirit is their best friend. He's not only with them; he speaks to them constantly. He tells them where to park their car, what to order for lunch, and where the best fishing spots are. Their lives are ruled by impressions.

Regardless of our awareness of God, his presence has always been a distinguishing characteristic of his people. God walked with Adam and Eve in the garden and dwelt with Israel through the tabernacle and temple. Moses told God it was his presence that would distinguish them from every other people on the face of the earth (Ex. 33:14–16). Near the end of the Old Testament, Ezekiel prophesied that when the temple was finally restored, the city where it was located would be called "The Lord Is There" (Ezek. 48:35). Jesus was Emmanuel, "God with us," and now dwells in us, both individually and corporately, by his Spirit (1 Cor. 3:16; 6:19). And one day we'll be in God's presence forever (Rev. 22:4–5).

It's not going too far to say that *our response to God's presence uniquely defines us as God's people.* Those who belong to God will cherish and pursue his presence. Psalm 105:4 encourages us,

> Seek the Lord and his strength;
>   seek his presence continually!

But how do we grow in our desire to encounter God's presence while maintaining an appreciation for the sufficiency of God's Word? What kind of encounters with God should we expect? Is it presumptuous to even talk about encounters and experiences with God?

131

The Bible describes four ways to think about God's presence that will help us answer those questions.

ACKNOWLEDGE GOD'S OMNIPRESENCE

Scripture tells us that God is present everywhere.

> Where shall I go from your Spirit?
>> Or where shall I flee from your presence?
> If I ascend to heaven, you are there!
>> If I make my bed in Sheol, you are there!
> If I take the wings of the morning
>> and dwell in the uttermost parts of the sea,
> even there your hand shall lead me,
>> and your right hand shall hold me. (Ps. 139:7–10)

There's no place we can be where God isn't. He knows all and sees all. "And no creature is hidden from his sight, but all are naked and exposed to the eyes of him to whom we must give account" (Heb. 4:13). God's omnipresence is one of the most mind-boggling assumptions of Scripture. There are plenty of times I wish I could be two places at once. God is not only two places at once; he's everywhere at once.

God can make his presence known anywhere and at any time, because he's already there.

EXPECT GOD'S PROMISED PRESENCE

God has also promised to be with us in a unique way on different occasions. His presence is especially promised to the church, which is "a dwelling place for God by the Spirit" (Eph. 2:22). God is with us to speak in power when his Word is preached (1 Cor. 2:4). As we celebrate the Lord's Supper, we're celebrating more than a reminder or a mere symbol. The risen Savior is present with us through faith as we remember his work of reconciliation. In a profound way we're being freshly strengthened in our union with him and with each other (1 Cor. 11:27–32).

Sometimes we're aware of God's promised presence, sometimes not. But trusting he's with us will produce specific results. We'll be comforted by his nearness. We'll be sobered by his awareness of all we're doing. We'll gain confidence in the midst of trying circumstances.

There are times, of course, when we become unexpectedly aware of the Lord's presence in an intense way. A sudden wave of peace comes over us. An irrepressible joy rises up from the depths of our soul. We experience the sweet sting of the Holy Spirit's conviction. In those moments, has God's presence come down to us? Have we been led into God's presence? No. God was present from the beginning. We've just become more aware of it.

D. A. Carson observes how "we often *feel* encouraged and edified" as we engage in corporate worship activities. The result is that "we are renewed in our awareness of God's love and God's truth, and we are encouraged to respond with adoration and action." Carson reminds us of this important truth: "Objectively, what brings us into the presence of God is the death and resurrection of the Lord Jesus." He warns that if we start thinking it's our worship activities that bring God's presence near, "it will not be long before we think of such worship as being meritorious, or efficacious, or the like."[4]

Carson is expressing concern for a mysticism that has always been a temptation for Christians. We reference drawing near to God with no mention of Christ or his finished work. It's an unmediated presence, something we can experience without an awareness of what Jesus did to make it possible. That kind of understanding leads us to start looking for the right combination, the right password, the right "secret" to experience God's presence again.

Maybe it was the way I lifted my hands.

It's always when we get to the chorus of that anointed song.

It happens every time Amanda sings.

Candles seem to help.

Let's be clear. No worship leader, pastor, or musician can bring us into the presence of God. It's not a certain prayer, a particular liturgy, a sacred object, the right bodily posture, or a certain mind-set. Only Jesus can lead us into God's presence, and he accomplished that through his substitutionary death, which forever removed the curtain of God's judgment that separated us from his presence (Heb. 10:19–22). It's only by putting our faith fully in Jesus's finished work of redemption that we can encounter the living God. Only Christ has truly brought us near to the Father.

We might become more aware of God's presence as we're singing to him, but he doesn't need music to make himself known to us. Harold Best describes the problem well: "Christian musicians . . . can create the impression that God is more present when music is being made than when it is not; that worship is more possible with music than without it; and that God might possibly depend on its presence before appearing."[5]

We can help our leaders in this area by not thanking them for "leading us into God's presence." Instead, we can thank them for their skillful leading, their musical ability, their planning, their enthusiasm, and their commitment to proclaiming God's Word and the gospel. Those are all means God uses to make us freshly aware of what Jesus has already done to bring us into God's presence.

So how do we tell the difference between actually experiencing and engaging with God's promised presence and simply being moved by a creative arrangement, a stunning vocal performance, a massive choir, or a beautiful melody? By examining what we're focusing on and its fruit. If all we can remember about an experience is how creative the instrumentation was or how awesome the lights were, we've most likely been emotionally moved but not spiritually changed. Encountering God generally bears the fruit of things like a greater hunger for his Word, a deeper love for the Savior, and a greater passion for a holy life. God can use music to affect us emotionally, but music will never mediate his presence. Only Jesus can do that.

The fact remains, however, that God has promised to dwell in the midst of his people. And that's a reality he wants us to benefit from *fully*.

PURSUE GOD'S EXPERIENCED PRESENCE

If God reveals his presence as he wills, does that leave any place for pursuing a greater manifestation of his presence? Should we hope to encounter God beyond taking it on faith that he's with us?

Absolutely. Consider these words from British pastor Graham Harrison:

There can be no substitute for that manifested presence of God which is always a biblical possibility for the people of God. When it is not being experienced they should humbly seek him for it, not neglecting their ongoing duties, nor denying their present blessings, but recognizing that there is always infinitely more with their God and Father who desires fellowship with those redeemed by the blood of his Son and regenerated by the work of his Spirit.[6]

Even though God is everywhere at once, he sometimes chooses to make his presence known. He appears to Moses in a burning bush (Ex. 3:2). He dwells with Israel in the tabernacle as they traverse through the wilderness (Ex. 29:42–45). He shakes the room in which the disciples are praying and displays his healing power through Peter's shadow (Acts 4:31; 5:15).

This side of heaven true worshipers will always long for a greater apprehension of and encounter with God and his character. We can be grateful for God's blessings and our present experiences of him, but still pray and long for greater manifestations of his power, glory, and beauty. And while we can't orchestrate the activity of God's Spirit, we can yearn for it, expect it, and be ready for it.

The example of the early church shows us that trusting in God's sovereignty doesn't preclude asking God to reveal his presence and power to us in demonstrable ways. At the end of Acts 4, the disciples expressed absolute confidence that God had been directing everything that had taken place up to that point. Herod, Pilate, the Gentiles, and the Jews all had done "whatever [God's] hand and [his] plan had predestined to take place" (4:28). But that in no way diminished the disciples' expectation that God would do wondrous things through them. "Stretch out your hand to heal," they prayed, so that more people would glorify Jesus (4:30). God's sovereignty is the foundation for expecting his active and experienced presence.

Genuine revivals are filled with countless examples of the living God visiting his people in presence and power. His normal activities increase in their intensity and scope. People are overcome by conviction of their sin, break down into tears, shake uncontrollably in the fear of God, and experience inexplicable peace and joy. Lukewarm Christians repent, sinners are converted, and ordinary activities are accompanied by extraordinary power. God reveals his presence for his glory. Why wouldn't we want to pursue similar works of God among us today?

Three attitudes that will help us in this pursuit are desperate dependence, eager expectation, and humble responsiveness.

Desperate Dependence

The first line of the hymn "Jesus Paid It All" reminds me of my constant state before God: "I hear the Savior say, 'Thy strength indeed is small.' "

Indeed it is. Sinful desires wage war against my heart (1 Pet. 2:11). The world constantly calls me to enjoy immoral pleasures, adopt ungodly attitudes, and live for passing rewards (1 John 2:15–17). The Devil prowls around like a roaring lion seeking someone to devour through deceit and condemnation (1 Pet. 5:8).

I am desperately dependent. And so are you.

God has sent his Spirit to help us. And the first thing the Spirit has done is given us God's Word. There we find "his precious and very great promises" (2 Pet. 1:4) and learn what God has done for us in the gospel, as well as how he has set us free to live. Dependence doesn't imply inactivity or simply waiting around. It's expressed in actively pursuing a deeper knowledge of God's ways and an impartation of his power through Scripture. It's the Word of God that revives our souls, makes us wise, fills our hearts with joy, and enlightens our eyes (Ps. 19:7–8). Ignoring the Bible not only is the opposite of being Spirit-led, but also shows that we trust ourselves more than God.

We also show our dependence on God by asking him to empower us by his Spirit. That's why we're taught to pray in and by the Spirit, and to pray for the Spirit's working (Rom. 8:26; Eph. 6:18; Jude 20). He helps us in our weakness. Jesus himself modeled a life of prayer when he was on earth. Paul told us that we are to "pray without ceasing" (1 Thess. 5:17). It's the height of presumption to think we can neglect prayer and still expect to experience God's presence and power. The root cause of our prayerlessness is often not laziness, but pride.

So, here's the question: How much do you pray for your church? For your times together? Do you pray specifically, asking the Spirit to reveal Christ to everyone gathered, to aid your leaders, to help the congregation sing with understanding, and to bring forth fruit in people's lives? Or do you unthinkingly toss up generic prayers like, "Bless everyone today, God"? Do you pray at all? What do you place more trust in: God's power, or the plans, performance, and personalities of people?

Consistently confessing our dependence on the Holy Spirit will produce a deep sense of gratitude, humility, and peace in our hearts. We'll see God answer our prayers. We'll remember that apart from Jesus we can do nothing. We'll be less tempted to think it's up to us. We'll realize God is actually in control, and we can't improve upon the job he's doing.

It's not our self-sufficiency that displays God's power, but our weakness (2 Cor. 12:9). And confessing that weakness is a sign that we desire to know more of God's presence.

Eager Expectation

At Thanksgiving some of my kids will drive nine hours with their families to spend the holiday with us. As the time approaches for their arrival, everyone's counting down the minutes, listening intently for the sound of a car turning into our cul-de-sac, watching carefully and eagerly for headlights moving across our front windows. We're anticipating they'll show up any minute.

Some of us say we want to encounter God, but we aren't expecting him to show up. We don't really think he'll do or say anything. We're like a parent opening a closet door to check whether the monster our child heard is really there. We appear to be expecting something, but we'd faint or scream if we found anything.

The Bible doesn't just tell us things we should believe about the Holy Spirit. It teaches us to have a posture of expectancy. And one of the things we should expect is that the Spirit will make God's presence known through various spiritual gifts. "Pursue love, and earnestly desire the spiritual gifts," Paul tells us in 1 Corinthians 14:1.

As we discussed previously, when we meet together the Spirit gives gifts, the Lord enables service, and God empowers a variety of activities. To each one a manifestation of the Spirit is given for the common good (1 Cor. 12:1–7). An aspect of that common good is giving evidence of God's presence in our midst. Do we expect God to be working in any and every spiritual gift?

When someone's running a sound board, they're exercising the gift of helps. As the offering plate is being passed, people are demonstrating the gift of giving. As the pastor preaches, the Spirit is moving upon our hearts through gifts of leadership and teaching. As someone prays for a friend battling cancer, they're functioning in the gift of mercy and possibly healing. Do we expect to encounter God in those moments?

Or do we keep our expectations low so we won't be disappointed? Do we tick through the different parts of our meetings like check boxes on a "to do" list?

Call to Worship? *Check.*

Songs? *Check.*

Prayer? *Check.*

Offering? *Check.*

Sermon? *Check.*

Communion? *Check.*

Benediction? *Gone.*

What if God was present to do great things in our hearts in every one of those moments? If we don't expect him to be active, we'll most likely miss what he's doing. We can expect great things from a great God who is dwelling in us and among us.

Humble Responsiveness

God's Spirit is always working to conform us to the image of Christ. It's an immense privilege to be his tool to accomplish that end in the lives of others as we exercise our spiritual gifts. But if we don't respond, we may miss out on the ways he wants to use us. As a result, we'll miss opportunities to build others up and experience the presence of the living God.

Often the work of the Spirit is despised because people follow the lead of the Corinthians and respond to it proudly. They view their own spiritual gifts as superior to others. They act as though their subjective experiences have objective authority. "The Lord told me" is an unwise way to begin any sentence, unless you're quoting Scripture. Subjective experiences don't have objective authority. But that doesn't mean we have to dismiss thoughts that come into our minds as bogus. We don't have to deny them or fear them.

Humble responsiveness means speaking up or acting whenever I think God might want to work through me. You might get the sudden urge to pray for someone as they mention they're probably going to lose their job. You notice someone you haven't seen in weeks and a Scripture "pops" into your mind. Humble responsiveness is making a point of sharing it with them right then or maybe giving them a call that afternoon.

In Sovereign Grace churches we typically provide a congregational microphone up front during the meetings. We anticipate the Spirit will lead members of the church to contribute a Scripture, prayer, or prophetic impression during our time together. A pastor screens what will be shared for its content and appropriateness. I've been in literally hundreds of meetings where God has used spontaneous contributions from people in the congregation to build up, stir up, and cheer up the saints (1 Cor. 14:3). And we experience God's presence as a result.

While we should expect to encounter God's presence when we gather, we can expect to encounter him at other times as well. Our faithful Shepherd at different times and in different ways confirms that he's lovingly and wisely watching over the details of our lives.

One time Julie and I were considering a potential move that no one else in the church knew about. Right before we finalized the decision, a friend stopped by our house with a written paragraph she thought might be an encouragement from the Lord for us. It had to do with making a major decision that involved some sadness but would result in much fruitfulness. My eyes welled up with tears of gratefulness.

Coincidence? Maybe. But something similar has happened many times. And each time it does, I experience God's particular care as individuals share specific and encouraging thoughts about things they have no knowledge of. Each time I become freshly aware of God's nearness and his kindness to us in Christ.

The Spirit's promptings don't always come in paragraph form. In fact, they rarely do. But for many of us, it can be difficult to believe that the Spirit would prompt us at all. Yet the New Testament contains numerous examples of God's intervention in daily life. Paul decides not to minister in Asia because the Holy Spirit forbids him (Acts 16:6). Philip has four unmarried daughters who prophesy (Acts 21:9). Agabus predicts that Paul will be bound and handed over to the Gentiles (Acts 21:11). The Thessalonians and Corinthians seem to experience the gift of spontaneous prophecy in their weekly gatherings (1 Cor. 14:29–32; 1 Thess. 5:19–21).

Sometimes we don't act on a thought for fear we might be wrong. But if what you do or share truly encourages someone, Jesus will be glorified and you'll both have a fresh awareness of God's presence. If it turns out your impression was irrelevant or wrong, you might be humbled. But the humble receive more grace (1 Pet. 5:5), so it's a win-win situation.

Nothing of what I'm describing here should lessen our commitment to the authority and sufficiency of God's Word. Experiences of God's presence, while important, aren't at the heart of our relationship with God. Theologian Andreas Köstenberger reminds us, "Biblical spirituality does not consist primarily of mystical, emotional experience, inward impressions and feelings, introspective meditation, or a monastic withdrawal from the world. The primary spiritual disciplines advocated by Scripture are prayer and the obedient study of God's Word."[7]

The right balance is captured in the words of D. A. Carson, who writes:

> We must desire to know more of God's presence in our lives, and pray for a display of unleashed, reforming, revivifying power among us, dreading all steps that aim to domesticate God. But such prayer and hunger must always be tempered with joyful submission to the constraints of biblical discipline.[8]

As you gladly submit to Scripture, who knows how God might minister to others through your humble response to what you believe to be the Spirit's promptings?

LONG FOR GOD'S UNVEILED PRESENCE

There's one more way we're to think about God's presence. Heaven. In heaven, there will be no temple to worship God in, no structure or locality that represents his presence more than another, because God and the Lamb will be the temple (Rev. 21:22).

In one sense, we can say we're experiencing God's presence in heaven right now. God has raised us up with Christ "and seated us with him in the heavenly places in Christ Jesus" (Eph. 2:6). The writer of Hebrews says that when we gather as the church, we're coming to

> the city of the living God, the heavenly Jerusalem, and to innumerable angels in festal gathering, and to the assembly of the firstborn who are enrolled in heaven, and to God, the judge of all, and to the spirits of the righteous made perfect, and to Jesus, the mediator of a new covenant, and to the sprinkled blood that speaks a better word than the blood of Abel. (Heb. 12:22–24)

Quite the church service! We join with the saints who have gone before us, rejoicing with them that death is not the final word for the Christian.

But the trials, deferred hopes, disappointments, losses, and tragedies of this life are an ever-present reminder: we're not home yet. The best is still to come. And what's still to come is what we'll consider in the final chapter.

TRUE WORSHIPERS *ANTICIPATE*

WORSHIP AND ETERNITY

No longer will there be anything accursed, but the throne
of God and of the Lamb will be in it, and his servants will
worship him. They will see his face, and his name will be on
their foreheads. And night will be no more. They will need
no light of lamp or sun, for the Lord God will be their light,
and they will reign forever and ever.

REVELATION 22:3–5

I've had the privilege of participating in meetings where the
magnificence of God's glory, or a profound awareness of
his mercy, made it difficult to remain standing. When that
happens, I'm aware that it is just the smallest glimpse, the
faintest whisper, of what awaits us in the new heavens and
the new earth.

No worship gathering in this life will ever rival the splen-
dor of what's to come.

WHAT ARE WE WAITING FOR?

What will worship in the coming age be like?

For starters, we'll never *not* be worshiping God. Every word, action, and thought will be offered up in pure devotion to the Savior who redeemed us for his own glory.

There will be no more arguments about instruments, songs, leaders, volume, video, dress, and doctrine. No distractions, hindrances, or rivals will hinder our love for God, because heaven is the place where God's will is done perfectly, immediately, and joyfully. It's where his will is always done. Heaven is filled with never-ending, ever-growing praise, thanksgiving, and worship to the one on the throne and the Lamb who was slain.

We can get so caught up in the debates surrounding worship in this life that we fail to learn from the Bible's description of worship in the next. It's easy to forget that what we're doing now is only an introduction, a foretaste, a shadow of what's to come. Our lives here are only the cover and title page to what lies ahead. For Christians, death begins "Chapter One of the Great Story," as C. S. Lewis writes, "which goes on forever: in which every chapter is better than the one before."[1]

Paul says we are to "look not to the things that are seen but to the things that are unseen" (2 Cor. 4:18). He refers to the "eternal weight of glory beyond all comparison" that awaits us. It's a weight of glory that makes our present sufferings seem light and momentary in comparison. Peter instructs his readers, "Set your hope fully on the grace that will be brought to you at the revelation of Jesus Christ" (1 Pet. 1:13). What does that glory and the grace that will be brought to us look like? And what difference should that make in our lives now?

The book of Revelation, along with a few other relevant passages, will help us answer those questions.

WHAT WILL HEAVEN BE LIKE?

Different Scriptures indicate that we're headed for a new city and better country that God has prepared for those who love him (Heb. 11:10, 16; 2 Pet. 3:13). It's likely we'll recognize places from this life, but they'll be freed from bondage to decay (Rom. 8:21). There'll be no more pain, tears, mourning, or death, because there'll be no more sin (Rev. 21:4). We won't need lights, lamps, or the sun because darkness won't exist. God himself will fill the universe with all the light we need (22:5). We'll experience the kind of life Adam and Eve knew in the garden of Eden, only better—richer, more beautiful, and never ending.

But the best part about heaven won't be the landscape, the activities, or the friends we'll recognize from this life. It will be finally beholding the face of the One who left his throne to redeem us. We'll look into his eyes and know instantly that no pleasure on earth compares with his love. We'll hear his voice singing over us and perhaps watch him create new worlds for us to rule over.

And we'll be with him. *With. Him.*

THE SAME, BUT DIFFERENT

In many ways the worship of the age to come will be similar to our worship on earth. Both are responses to God's revelation of himself, celebrating his Word, works, and worthiness

(Rev. 5:9–10; 16:4–7; 19:1–5). Both center on the glories of the Lamb who has "ransomed people for God / from every tribe and language and people and nation" (Rev. 5:9). Both are marked by full engagement and find their fulfillment in worshiping together as the people of God in God's presence (Rev. 4:10; 5:9, 11, 13; 7:11; 21:3). In these and other ways, the worship of earth anticipates and reflects the worship of heaven.

But there will be significant differences.

In heaven, we'll be in the actual, unveiled presence of God. While we can encounter God's presence in this life, the Bible speaks of heaven as a place where God is uniquely present. The angel Gabriel informs a frightened Mary, "I stand in the presence of God." The writer of Hebrews tells us, "Christ has entered . . . into heaven itself, now to appear in *the presence of God* on our behalf" (Heb. 9:24). Wayne Grudem comments:

> We might find it misleading to say that God is "more present" in heaven than anywhere else, but it would not be misleading to say that God is present in a special way in heaven, present especially there to bless and to show forth his glory. We could also say that God manifests his presence more fully in heaven than elsewhere.[2]

In this life, our experience of God's presence is limited by what God chooses to show us and what we can perceive. In the New Jerusalem, God's complete and immediate presence will be everywhere. We will live, breathe, eat, sing, work, and rest forever in the Most Holy Place, where God's presence always dwells.

In heaven, we won't have to confess our sin, evangelize the lost, or seek justice for the oppressed. While we'll be forever aware of our need for a Savior in heaven, God will never again bring up our sins. Our worship won't have to be "evangelistic" because there'll be no one who doesn't know the Lord. We won't have to stand up for those who are suffering at the hands of others because there will be no more injustice, tyranny, or oppression. We won't have children to keep in line, relational conflicts to work through, or despairing thoughts to battle. Poverty in all its forms will be eradicated, and every person will know the love of Christ that surpasses all knowledge (Eph. 3:19).

In heaven, we'll worship God with glorified bodies. My physical strength seems to be deteriorating weekly. But one day God will remove every aspect of weakness in our bodies. Sharper eyes will enjoy greater beauty, brighter minds will perceive deeper wisdom, and clearer ears will make every sound more glorious. Our vocal cords won't get hoarse from singing. Our legs won't get tired from standing or dancing. Our arms will never grow tired from lifting them in praise. Maybe some Christians will lift them for the first time! We'll be able to grasp and respond to God's greatness like never before.

David Powlison explains it like this: "Everything that is now incomplete, semi-conscious, tainted, and half-baked will then be complete, clear-minded, holy, and utterly fulfilled. We and God will inherit each other, will possess each other, will share together in His glory. We live in this hope."[3]

For a long time I thought we wouldn't learn anything in heaven, that we'd arrive and instantly know all we'd ever know.

But God saved us so that "in the coming ages he might show the *immeasurable* riches of his grace in kindness toward us in Christ Jesus" (Eph. 2:7). "Immeasurable" means we'll never reach the end. Like a multifaceted diamond, God will display fresh aspects of his character, power, and love, and in response we'll offer up new songs of praise, exaltation, and thanksgiving.

In heaven, there will be no separation between adoration and action. One of the challenges we face on earth is the disconnect between worship as an event and worship as every moment. While we understand that worship is something we do in all of life, we're constantly tempted to view Sunday mornings as "true" worship. We end up seeking to recharge our spiritual batteries on Sundays, struggling the rest of the week to be aware of God's presence in the mundane affairs of life. That won't be a problem in heaven. God will be supreme in our thoughts, attitudes, motives, actions, and words.

The book of Revelation indicates there will still be times of gathered praise, when we'll purposefully proclaim the glories of the Lamb who redeemed us for the Father's glory. But our worship at other times will be no less focused or intentional. Every choice and action will be shaped and compelled by a desire to delight in, magnify, and draw attention to the Savior. Idolatry will no longer be a problem because everything that competes for God's glory in our hearts will be brought into subjection to Jesus Christ (1 Cor. 15:24–28; Rev. 19:1–3). All our idols will be finally and completely toppled.

In heaven, our knowledge of God will be no longer by faith but by sight. In this life, whatever doesn't proceed from faith is sin. God commands us to stand firm in our faith, tells us we can't please him without faith, and commands us to walk by faith and not sight (Rom. 14:22; 1 Cor. 16:13; 2 Cor. 5:7; Heb. 11:6). Worshiping God in the here and now requires faith.

We know Jesus is the only Lord, but we don't yet see every knee bowing before him. We know God is sovereign and good—but children die, malicious dictators rise to power, and sin continues to ravage and destroy. Jesus promised he would return to establish his kingdom, but right now the world seems to grow colder, darker, and more hopeless with each passing generation. That's why we need faith. It's the assurance of things we hope for and the conviction about things we can't see (Heb. 11:1).

But in heaven we won't have to hope any more. We'll have every good thing we've ever hoped for, and more. All our God-honoring dreams, ambitions, and desires will be fulfilled beyond our wildest imagination. And as far as the things we can't see now—well, that won't be a problem either. We'll finally gaze on what our eyes have longed to behold more than anything—the face of God.

WHAT DIFFERENCE DOES IT MAKE?

God has given us glimpses of heaven not only to make us long for more of them, but also to be changed by them. Our church services and lives may not seem very heavenly at the moment, but there is an undeniable connection between what's to come and the present age. It is right, comforting, and immeasurably helpful to meditate on what awaits us, made possible through the atoning work of our glorious Savior.

Here are three specific ways that reflecting on the worship of heaven helps and changes us.

Reflecting on the worship of heaven opens our eyes to the cosmic battle for true worship. The book of Revelation portrays God's enemies in the most offensive ways possible to communicate the true nature of our choices. John uses words like "beast," "abomination," "prostitute," "dragon," and "serpent" to describe the satanic forces that compete with God for our worship (Rev. 11:7; 17:5; 19:2; 20:2). In various ways they serve as a counterfeit to Christ and try to turn our hearts against him.

If we fully understand what's at stake when we talk about worship, we'll have a hard time treating it casually. We are given only two choices in life—to worship God or idols. There are no other options. And to worship anything but God is rebellion against his rule and a rejection of his sovereign love.

Life on earth is not meaningless. Our decisions reflect our worship. Every person is constantly making choices for God or against him. We are exalting either the only Savior of the world or something else. No one can maintain neutrality. There is no imaginary fence we can straddle. Heaven shows us there is a clear line between those who gladly recognize the sovereignty and mercy of God and the Lamb, and those who follow the beast and the dragon. David Peterson writes:

> Acceptable worship involves acknowledging and accepting God's claim for exclusive devotion and loyalty by rejecting every alternative. In the market-place, in politics, in the

field of education or the arts, the Christian is constantly challenged to make the decisive choice for God that Jesus himself made, when he was tested so forcefully in the wilderness (*cf.* Mt. 4:8–10).[4]

Corporate worship is a regular opportunity to remind ourselves of the forces arrayed against God's people, forces constantly seeking to rule our affections, thoughts, and choices. It is also the time to remember we serve an omnipotent God who will crush all opposition to his reign. Isaiah prophesies about that day when

> the haughtiness of man shall be humbled,
> > and the lofty pride of men shall be brought low,
> > and the LORD alone will be exalted in that day.
> And the idols shall utterly pass away. (Isa. 2:17–18)

God's preview of heaven assures us that day is coming.

Reflecting on the worship of heaven causes us to pursue holiness. In his first letter, John writes: "Beloved, we are God's children now, and what we will be has not yet appeared; but we know that when he appears we shall be like him, because we shall see him as he is. And everyone who thus hopes in him purifies himself as he is pure" (1 John 3:2–3). Why is that? How does knowing that God will make us like himself in the future motivate us to change now?

Our destination ultimately determines our path. If you have repented of your sins and trusted in the atoning death of Christ, God has reserved a place for you among heaven's sinless, spotless saints. You will be clothed in a white robe, made clean by the blood of the Lamb (Rev. 7:13–14). There's nothing we can do to earn heaven, nor will we ever attain perfection in this life. But our future is certain. We will no longer be marred or weighed down by our sin. We will trust completely and constantly in the one who is called "Faithful and True" (Rev. 19:11).

If that's what heaven is going to be like, it only makes sense to pursue that life now. People who want to sin as much as they can before they die because "everything will be forgiven" at that point don't understand the nature or joy of salvation. God saves us not only from the flames of hell, but also from the hellish desires within us that blind us to his goodness.

No one in heaven will want to be sexually immoral, steal someone else's property, or criticize the person standing next to them. Temptation will be a thing of the past because we will know that absolutely nothing is better than knowing God. Everything we enjoy then—sights, smells, sounds, and activities—we will enjoy because of God. Every sin will be finally vanquished through the victorious work of Jesus Christ. We will be holy.

Heaven won't be a place where God pours out his love on those who never wanted it. Heaven is for those whose greatest desire in this life is to know and be like the Savior who redeemed them. The age to come won't be the opposite of what we seek now, but the fulfillment of it. So we pursue holiness.

Reflecting on the worship of heaven fills us with joy and confidence in the midst of suffering. John wrote the book of Revelation to Christians undergoing intense persecution, even being martyred for their faith. John himself had been exiled to the island of Patmos apparently because he had refused to worship the Roman emperor. False teachers were causing confusion in churches and leading them astray. Worse, leaders were putting up with them. Christianity was just slightly more than half a century old. The future didn't look promising.

How would the church worship God? Where would they find the strength to boldly confess their faith and continue to preach the gospel? In the midst of their trials, God sent "the revelation of Jesus Christ" to the apostle John. And at the center of that revelation was a throne. While the Roman emperor demanded worship and homage from his subjects, he was unaware of another King on a higher throne. This throne commanded the worship not only of the Roman Empire but of every creature in heaven and on earth and under the earth (Rev. 5:13).

In every age God's people are called to suffer for the sake of the gospel. God promises that all who desire to live a godly life in Christ Jesus will be persecuted (2 Tim. 3:12). As a Christian living in twenty-first-century America, I haven't known pronounced persecution. But hundreds of thousands of Christians have. I've met pastors in other countries who endure physical violence and potential death because of their faith. Their example, along with others' I've known or read about, inspires and humbles me.

Whatever form persecution takes—inconvenience, verbal abuse, rejection, or martyrdom—our temptation will be to abandon our trust in God and turn to false gods for protection. The worship portrayed in the book of Revelation answers every question that may rise in our hearts during such a time, assuring us that "the kingdom of the world has become the kingdom of our Lord and of his Christ, and he shall reign forever and ever" (Rev. 11:15).

Every knee will bow before Jesus, the King of kings and Lord of lords; Jesus, the root and descendant of David, the Creator of David's life and fruit of his offspring; Jesus, the bright and morning star that will never fade or diminish, that will only grow brighter, stronger, clearer, and more dazzling throughout all eternity; Jesus, the eternal Savior whose sacrifice is sufficient to rescue people from every corner of the globe throughout all history (Rev. 5:9; 19:16; 22:16).

This Jesus will be worshiped by all creation for the glory of the Father through the power of the Holy Spirit—forever.

LOOKING FORWARD

But for now, we wait. Like a baby in the womb, we're getting ready for a continuation of our present life that is different in unimaginable ways. In one sense we're already enjoying the benefits of the age to come. But there's so much that still awaits us.

To a not-yet-born baby, life is essentially dark, wet, and cramped. But those nine months, with all their changes, growth, and adjustments, represent a time of preparation, not the final destination. And as with a newborn child, one day our eyes will open up to see a panorama so startling it will leave us gasping for grace-drenched air. Our final moment on earth won't be the last stop on the train of our existence. In light of eternity, we'll be stepping off the platform at the boarding station.

Heaven teaches us that God doesn't hand out all his riches in this life. Whatever experiences God grants us of his glory now, we'll always be left wanting more. That's the way God intended it to be. That "more" awaits us in the next life.

That's one of the reasons we're commanded to celebrate the Lord's Supper "until he comes" (1 Cor. 11:26). Even as we feast at his table and proclaim the Lord's death that reconciled us to God, our eyes are on the future wedding feast. We're among those who "have loved his appearing" (2 Tim. 4:8) because we recognize that our citizenship is in heaven.

Noel Due describes this hope well:

> We look forward to that day when the great multitude stand in the nearer presence of Father, filled to all the fullness of God the Spirit, through whom they are united with the Son. There they will look around and within, and find only worship. Despite all the attacks of the evil one, the drag of indwelling sin and the seductive power of the idols throughout their long history, their song will be one of praise drenched with wonder. In them the commandment will be completely fulfilled: they will have no other God but him. And in them the promise will be fully realized: he is their God and they are his people.[5]

Words are inadequate to express the awe, adoration, and joy that fill our hearts as we consider the unshakeable, unmovable, uninterrupted confidence of heaven and the Savior who has made it all possible.

THE FINAL FEAST

Every person who has trusted in Christ will be an honored attendee at the marriage supper of the Lamb. Looking around, we'll be amazed to see table after table, stretching endlessly beyond what our eyes can make out. Men and women of every background, ethnicity, and nation will be eating, laughing, perhaps singing, awash in peace, joy, and an overwhelming sense of loving and being loved.

We'll notice people whose faith we questioned in this life. Individuals who irritated us, who seemed immature, who actually made our life harder. We'll see people we thought had no shot of sitting at this table. And before any shred of self-righteous judgment rises up in our hearts, we'll be rendered speechlessly grateful.

Because you and I had no shot of sitting at this table. But we're there, each of us an undeserving guest made fit by the Bridegroom. We've been made fit after blindly rebelling against God's right to rule us; made fit after pursuing our own ways and wisdom; made fit after choosing to run away from God rather than to him; made fit after being ruled by death, despair, madness, and misery for thousands of years.

But in his great kindness, God sent his Son, Jesus Christ, to bring us back to himself and to redeem us from all that would destroy us. It's a work of grace and mercy from beginning to end, rooted in eternity past and to be enjoyed for endless ages, for the glory of the Father, Son, and Holy Spirit. Therefore, "as it is written, 'Let the one who boasts, boast in the Lord'" (1 Cor. 1:31).

True worshipers hold fast to the hope that one day we will do nothing *but* boast in the Lord. For we consider it the great end of our existence to find ourselves numbered among the worshipers of God.

There can be no higher purpose.

There can be no greater joy.

And for those who have gratefully received God's mercy in Jesus Christ, there can be no other end.

NOTES

Chapter 1: True Worshipers *Matter*: Worship and Reality

1. Some of the books I've found most helpful are David Peterson, *Engaging with God: A Biblical Theology of Worship* (Grand Rapids, MI: Eerdmans, 1992); Vaughan Roberts, *True Worship* (Waynesboro, GA: Authentic Media, 2002); D. A. Carson, ed., *Worship by the Book* (Grand Rapids, MI: Zondervan, 2002); Bryan Chapell, *Christ-Centered Worship: Letting the Gospel Shape Our Practice* (Grand Rapids, MI: Baker Academic, 2009); Harold Best, *Unceasing Worship: Biblical Perspectives on Worship and the Arts* (Downers Grove, IL: InterVarsity Press, 2003); and Mike Cosper, *Rhythms of Grace: How the Church's Worship Tells the Story of the Gospel* (Wheaton, IL: Crossway, 2013).

2. John Calvin, *Commentary on the Book of Psalms* (vol. 2), in *Calvin's Commentaries*, vol. 5, trans. James Anderson (Grand Rapids: Baker, 1996), at Ps. 52:8.

3. The italicized are excerpts from John 4:7–23.

4. Carson, *Worship by the Book*, 37.

Chapter 2: True Worshipers *Receive*: Worship and Our Inability

1. An excellent introduction to the Trinity that explores God's triune relationships and their impact on us is Michael Reeves, *Delighting in the Trinity: An Introduction to the Christian Faith* (Downers Grove, IL: InterVarsity Press, 2012).

2. D. A. Carson, ed., *Worship by the Book* (Grand Rapids, MI: Zondervan, 2002), 34.

3. Horatio G. Spafford, "It Is Well with My Soul" (1873).

4. Derek Kidner, *Psalms 73–150*, Tyndale Old Testament Commentaries (Downers Grove, IL: InterVarsity Press, 1975), 401.

5. Vaughan Roberts, *True Worship* (Waynesboro, GA: Authentic Media, 2002), 16.

6. John Stott, *The Contemporary Christian: Applying God's Word to Today's World* (Downers Grove, IL: InterVarsity Press, 1995), 174.

7. Timothy Ward, *Words of Life: Scripture as the Living and Active Word of God* (Downers Grove, IL: InterVarsity Press, 2009), 32.

8. Michael Horton, *A Better Way: Rediscovering the Drama of Christ-Centered Worship* (Grand Rapids, MI: Baker, 2002), 26.

9. A few books I'd recommend for use along with your Bible are the *ESV Study Bible*, ed. Wayne Grudem et al. (Wheaton, IL: Crossway, 2008); Wayne Grudem, *Systematic Theology: An Introduction to Biblical Doctrine* (Grand Rapids, MI: Zondervan, 1995); J. I. Packer, *Knowing God* (Downers Grove, IL: InterVarsity Press, 1973); D. A. Carson, *For the Love of God: A Daily Companion for Discovering the Riches of God's Word*, 2 vols. (Wheaton, IL: Crossway, 1998, 2006); J. I. Packer, *Concise Theology: A Guide to Historic Christian Beliefs* (Wheaton, IL: Tyndale House, 1993); Michael Reeves, *Delighting in the Trinity: An Introduction to the Christian Faith* (Downers Grove, IL: InterVarsity Press, 2012); Kevin DeYoung, *Taking God at His Word: Why the Bible Is Knowable, Necessary, and Enough, and What That Means for You and Me* (Wheaton, IL: Crossway, 2014); Vaughan Roberts, *God's Big Picture: Tracing the Storyline of the Bible* (Downers Grove, IL: InterVarsity Press, 2002); John Piper, *Desiring God: Meditations of a Christian Hedonist*, rev. ed. (Colorado Springs: Multnomah, 2011); and many more.

10. Charles Spurgeon, sermon 542, on 2 Tim. 4:13, http://www
    .spurgeon.org/sermons/0542.htm.

Chapter 3: True Worshipers *Exalt*: Worship and Humility

1. Matt Papa, "Look & Live (Worship or Die)," http://www
   .mattpapa.com/2013/10/look-live-worship-or-die/.
2. David Peterson, in *Worship: Adoration and Action*, ed. D. A.
   Carson (Grand Rapids, MI: Baker, 1993), 52.
3. See David Peterson, "Honouring, Serving and Respecting
   God," chap. 2 in *Engaging with God: A Biblical Theology of
   Worship* (Grand Rapids, MI: Eerdmans, 1992), for a fuller
   treatment of worship vocabulary in Scripture.
4. For an in-depth discussion of how Job glorified God in his
   suffering, see Tim Keller, "Praying," chap. 14 in *Walking with
   God through Pain and Suffering* (New York: Dutton, 2013).
5. From the prayer "The Awakened Sinner," in *The Valley of Vision*, ed. Arthur Bennett (Edinburgh: Banner of Truth, 1975),
   36; language modernized.
6. 1 Chron. 16:8; Pss. 30:4; 97:12; 100:4; 136:1–3; Col. 3:17;
   1 Thess. 5:18.
7. "Already and not yet" is a phrase originally popularized by
   theologian George Eldon Ladd (1911–1982).
8. I discuss the categories of Word, worthiness, and works more
   fully in "Magnifies the Greatness of God," chap. 8 in Bob
   Kauflin, *Worship Matters: Leading Others to Encounter the
   Greatness of God* (Wheaton, IL: Crossway, 2008).
9. An excellent book that explores the different ways Jesus has
   served us and motivates grace-empowered serving is John
   Hindley, *Serving without Sinking: How to Serve Christ and
   Keep Your Joy* (Purcellville, VA: Good Book, 2013).

Chapter 4: True Worshipers *Gather*: Worship and Community

1. Iain M. Duguid, "Old Testament Worship Theology," course
   syllabus, Grove City College, 14.

2. Bryan Chapell, *Christ-Centered Worship: Letting the Gospel Shape Our Practice* (Grand Rapids, MI: Baker Academic, 2009), 120.

3. Ex. 20:2; Deut. 4:34; Neh. 9:9; Pss. 78:51; 81:10; 105:23, 37; 135:8; Jer. 32:20.

4. Duguid, "Old Testament Worship Theology," 73.

5. Mark Dever, *The Church: The Gospel Made Visible* (Nashville, TN: B&H Academic, 2012), xi.

6. Donald Whitney, *Spiritual Disciplines within the Church: Participating Fully in the Body of Christ* (Chicago: Moody, 1996), 77.

Chapter 5: True Worshipers *Edify*: Worship and Maturity

1. Bryan Chapell, *Christ-Centered Worship: Letting the Gospel Shape Our Practice* (Grand Rapids, MI: Baker Academic, 2009), 119.

2. The idea for these headings originated in a message by my friend Jeff Purswell, called "The Pastor and the Spirit," given at the Together for the Gospel conference in 2012.

3. David Prior, *The Message of 1 Corinthians: Life in the Local Church* (Downers Grove, IL: InterVarsity Press, 1985), 214.

4. David Garland, *1 Corinthians*, Baker Exegetical Commentary on the New Testament (Grand Rapids, MI: Baker, 2003), 596.

Chapter 6: True Worshipers *Sing*: Worship and Music

1. Harold Best, *Unceasing Worship: Biblical Perspectives on Worship and the Arts* (Downers Grove, IL: InterVarsity Press, 2003), 144–45.

2. C. S. Lewis, "On Church Music," in Lewis, *Christian Reflections*, ed. Walter Hooper (Grand Rapids, MI: Eerdmans, 1995), 96.

3. Everett Ferguson, *The Church of Christ: A Biblical Ecclesiology for Today* (Grand Rapids, MI: Eerdmans, 1997), 269.

4. Oliver W. Sacks, *Musicophilia: Takes of Music and the Brain* (New York: Knopf, 2007), 237.

5. These lines come from Reginald Heber, "Holy, Holy, Holy" (1826), Matt and Beth Redman, "Blessed Be Your Name" (2005), Charitie Lees Bancroft, "Before the Throne of God Above" (1863), and "Be Thou My Vision," trans. Eleanor Hull (1912).

6. Douglas Moo, "Informed Worship," *Tabletalk*, October 2002.

7. John Piper, from the sermon "Singing and Making Melody to the Lord," *desiringGod* blog, December 28, 1997, http://www.desiringgod.org/sermons/singing-and-making-melody-to-the-lord.

8. Isaac Watts, "Toward the Improvement of Psalmody," in *The Works of the Rev. Isaac Watts, D.D.*, 9 vols. (London, 1813), 9:30.

9. See also 1 Chron. 16:33; Job 29:13; Ps. 63:7; Isa. 12:6; Jer. 51:48.

10. John R. W. Stott, *The Living Church: Convictions of a Lifelong Pastor* (Downers Grove, IL: InterVarsity Press, 2007), 37.

11. John Calvin, *Commentary on the Acts of the Apostles* (vol. 2) in *Calvin's Commentaries*, vol. 19, trans. Henry Beveridge (Grand Rapids: Baker, 1996), at Acts 20:36.

Chapter 7: True Worshipers *Keep Singing*: Worship and Perseverance

1. Jonathan Edwards, *A Treatise concerning Religious Affections* (Boston: Kneeland and Green, 1746), part 1, sec. 2 (". . . that true religion . . . consists in the affections"), point 9.

2. Isaac Watts, *A Guide to Prayer* (Carlisle, PA: Banner of Truth, 2001), 28.

Chapter 8: True Worshipers *Encounter*: Worship and the Presence of God

1. Robert Rayburn, *O Come Let Us Worship* (Grand Rapids, MI: Baker, 1980), 22.

2. J. I. Packer, *Keep in Step with the Spirit* (Old Tappan, NJ: Revell, 1984), 47, 49.

3. Wayne Grudem, *Systematic Theology: An Introduction to Biblical Doctrine* (Grand Rapids, MI: Zondervan, 1995), 641.

4. D. A. Carson, "Worship under the Word," chap. 1 in *Worship by the Book*, ed. D. A. Carson (Grand Rapids, MI: Zondervan, 2002), 50–51.

5. Harold M. Best, *Music through the Eyes of Faith* (New York: HarperOne, 1993), 153.

6. Graham Harrison, "Worship and the Presence of God," *Banner of Truth* blog, April 19, 2002, http://banneroftruth.org/us/resources/articles/2002/worship-and-the-presence-of-god.

7. Andreas J. Köstenberger, *Excellence: The Character of God and the Pursuit of Scholarly Virtue* (Wheaton, IL: Crossway, 2011), Kindle locations 348–50.

8. D. A. Carson, *Showing the Spirit: A Theological Exposition of 1 Corinthians 12–14* (Grand Rapids, MI: Baker, 1987), 188.

Chapter 9: True Worshipers *Anticipate*: Worship and Eternity

1. C. S. Lewis, *The Last Battle*, The Chronicles of Narnia (New York: HarperCollins, 1994), 228.

2. Wayne Grudem, *Systematic Theology: An Introduction to Biblical Doctrine* (Grand Rapids, MI: Zondervan, 1995), 176.

3. David Powlison, "Who Is God?," *The Journal of Biblical Counseling* 17, no. 2 (1999): 23.

4. David Peterson, *Engaging with God: A Biblical Theology of Worship* (Grand Rapids, MI: Eerdmans, 1992), 265.

5. Noel Due, *Created for Worship: From Genesis to Revelation to You* (Fearn, Ross-shire, UK: Christian Focus, 2005), 238.

GENERAL INDEX

General Index

Due, Noel, 157
Duguid, Iain, 71, 77

eager expectation, 139–40
Eden, 32–33, 147
edification, in worship, 84–95
Edwards, Jonathan, 117
emotionalism, 108, 115
emotions
  in song, 106, 107–9, 116–17
  in worship, 28, 41–42
encountering God, in worship, 128–43
encouragement, 64, 85
  through song, 110
eternal life, 37
eternity, 21–22
evangelism, 67
exalting God, 51–68, 115
exiles, returning from Babylon, 99
exodus, 34, 98

face of God, 147, 151
faith, 57–58
faith and sight, 150–51
fall, 33
Father, seeking true worshipers, 26, 27
fears, 109
fellowship, 78
filled with the Spirit, 102
Fishnet, 19–20
forgiveness, 68

Garland, David, 89
gathered church, raised up to heaven, 144
gathering for worship, 69–83
gentleness, 56
gifts, 76
  variety of, 87–90
GLAD (Christian group), 96
glorified bodies, 149
God
  answers prayer, 139
  character of, 57–58
  faithfulness of, 57
  glory visible in worship, 80–81
  jealous for his own glory, 52

presence of, 28, 76–77, 128–43
  in Eden, 33
  in heaven, 143–44, 148
  sovereignty of, 51, 136
  wisdom of, 57, 80
godly speech, 64–65
good works, 68
gospel, in worship, 74, 93–95
grace, 39, 47–48, 158
  in corporate gatherings, 76
  immeasurable riches of, 150
gratefulness, 58–59, 62, 94, 123, 138
"great end of existence," 21–22
greed, 62
Grudem, Wayne, 130, 148

Hamilton, Alexander, 127–28
Harrison, Graham, 135–36
heart, in worship, 122–23
  in singing, 111, 116, 117
heaven
  unity in, 113
  worship in, 143–44, 145–59
heavenly Jerusalem, 144
heresy, 43
holiness, 153–54
Holy Spirit
  gifts of, 139–40
  illumination of, 46
  and prayer, 138
  and presence of God, 129–30
  as stimulant for song, 103
  and Word of God, 39, 44–45
hope, 58, 151
horizontal focus of worship, 28, 105
Horton, Michael, 44
Hughes, Tim, 108
humble responsiveness, 140–43
humility, 56, 138
hypocrisy, in singing, 119–21

idolatry, 28, 50–51, 120, 150, 152
individualism, 87
instrumentation, 124–25, 135
intelligibility, in worship, 92–93
Israel
  idolatry of, 35

SCRIPTURE INDEX

Also Available from Bob Kauflin

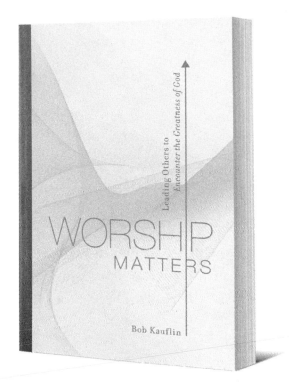

"*Worship Matters* will inspire you as a worshiper and spur you on as a leader of worship."

MATT REDMAN, lead worshiper and songwriter, Brighton, UK

"Bob's approach is humble, yet authoritative; comprehensive, yet inspirational. And if you take his gentle but clear teaching onboard, it will help make you fully equipped in mind, heart, and spirit to lead others in worship."

STUART TOWNEND, Christian songwriter

Download a free study guide
for *True Worshipers* at
crossway.org/TrueWorshipersSG